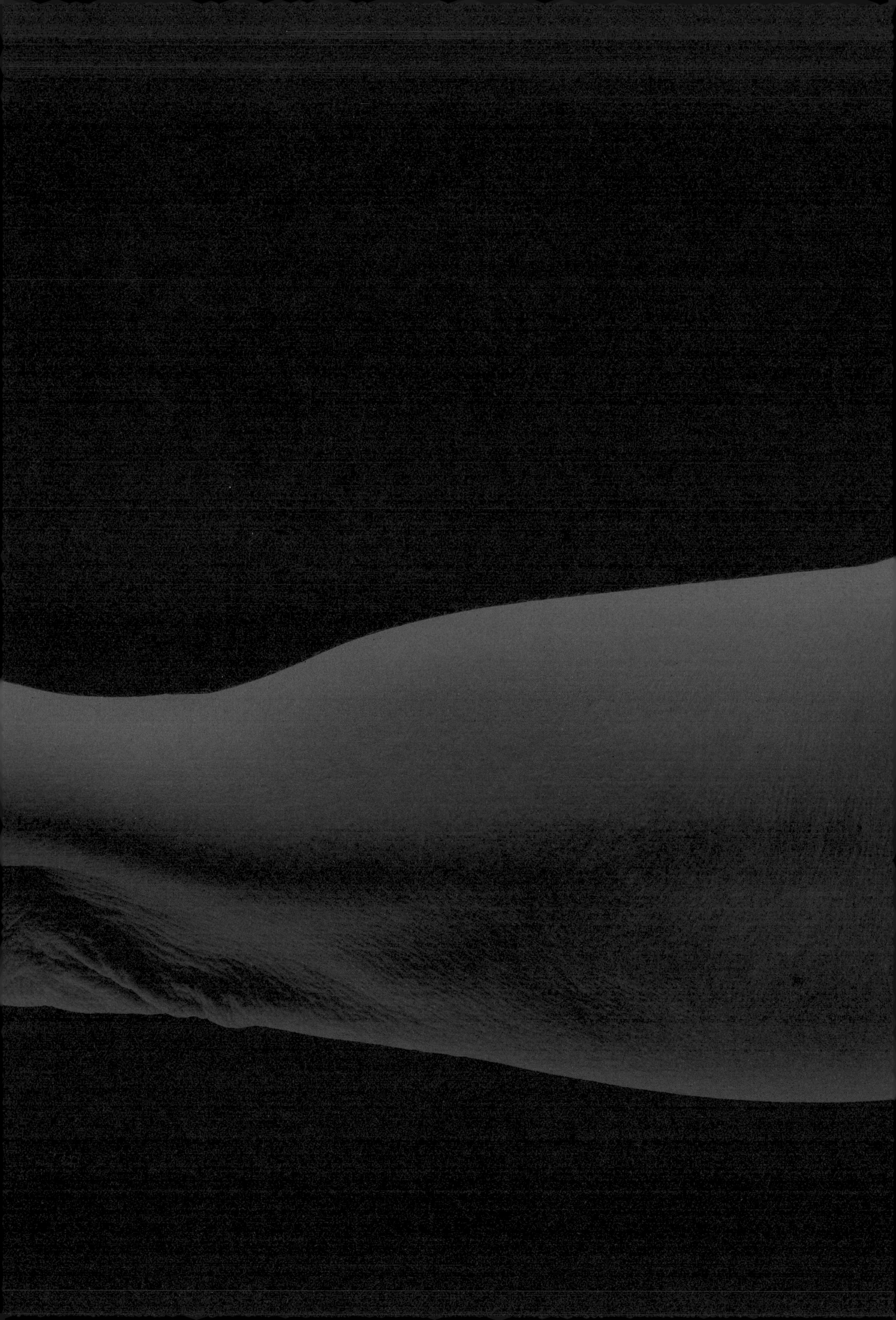

# Jesse Jones

# TREMBLE TREMBLE

# THE TOWER

Talbot Rice Gallery

This catalogue is published on the occasion of Jesse Jones' exhibition *The Tower*, 24 June – 30 September 2023

Talbot Rice Gallery
University of Edinburgh

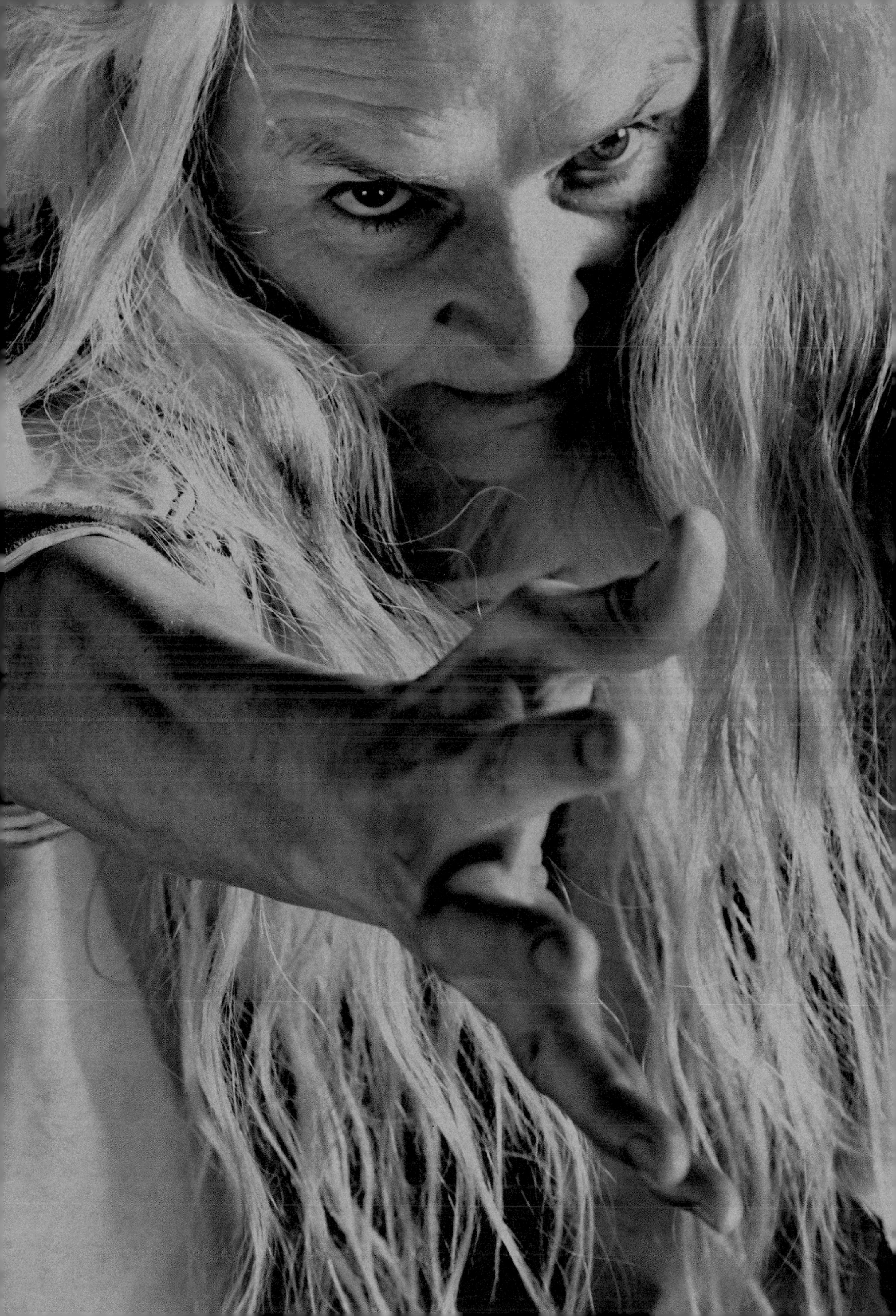

# Introduction

Tessa Giblin

Jesse Jones' work has developed alongside seismic shifts in Ireland's cultural and political landscape. Jones' research that first gave rise to *Tremble Tremble* and then *The Tower* is grounded in the history of female mystical thought as a site of autonomy and resistance. She trusts in the potential of art to ignite our collective imaginary and agitate for change against the centuries of capital accumulation that has impacted upon women's freedoms.

This book unpacks these two artworks to demonstrate that this vision is rooted in a deep interrogation of the cultural and political histories that swirl around them. It is also the story about Jones' motivation as an artist and the extraordinary sea of change that has engulfed Ireland over the past decade. During our interview in May 2023 (which falls at the end of this book), Jones said: 'An artist's work can connect to something very deep within our culture, which is our shared experience and ability to articulate a sense of the unknown, a sense of the troubling of what the potential futures are or what the past is. And it is artists who do this troubling. They do the kind of work of the unconscious that is necessary for us to have a rational political, collective strategy.' In this, she expresses a belief in art that we both share, and that has been the foundation of more than a decade of artistic and exhibition-making conversations between us.

This 'troubling' connects to the core of how we perceive the world and art's power to provide critical platforms for public debate. Reflecting upon Jones' magnificent body of work, I continue to marvel at her synthesis of politics and aesthetics, histories and imaginaries, evidence and hypotheses. We are honoured to celebrate an artist who is able to use this magic to catalyse the project of female emancipation.

Having shown both *Tremble Tremble* and *The Tower* at Talbot Rice Gallery we have witnessed the impact they made on public audiences and students alike, reinforcing transformative public debate. In short, Jesse Jones' work has affected the character of the gallery's programme as much as we have carried her forward. To publish this book with Edinburgh University Press stands as a testament to the character that pervades this era of Talbot Rice Gallery's programming, driven by the principle that art is not separate from the world around us.

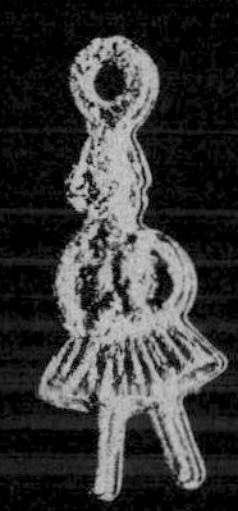

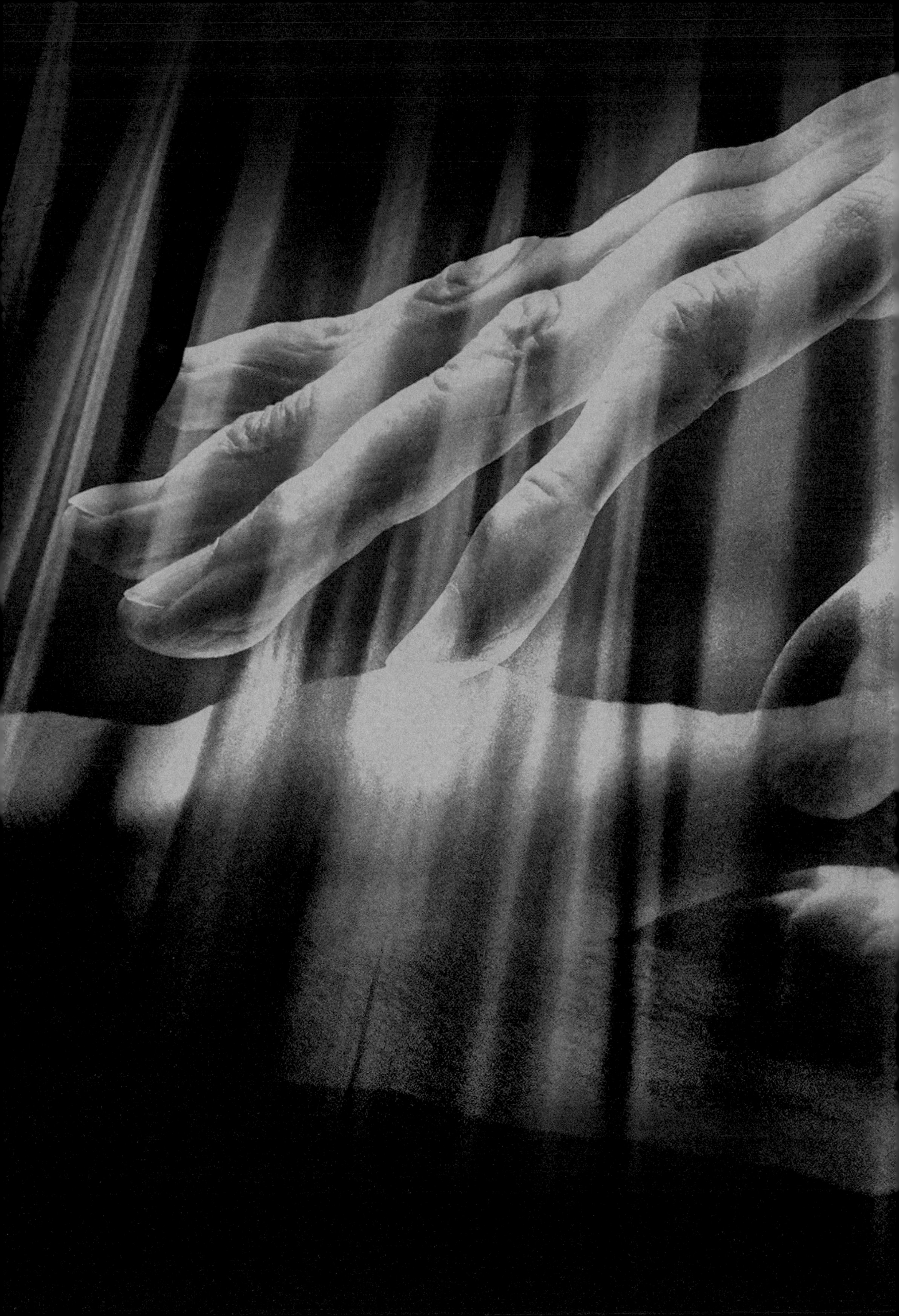

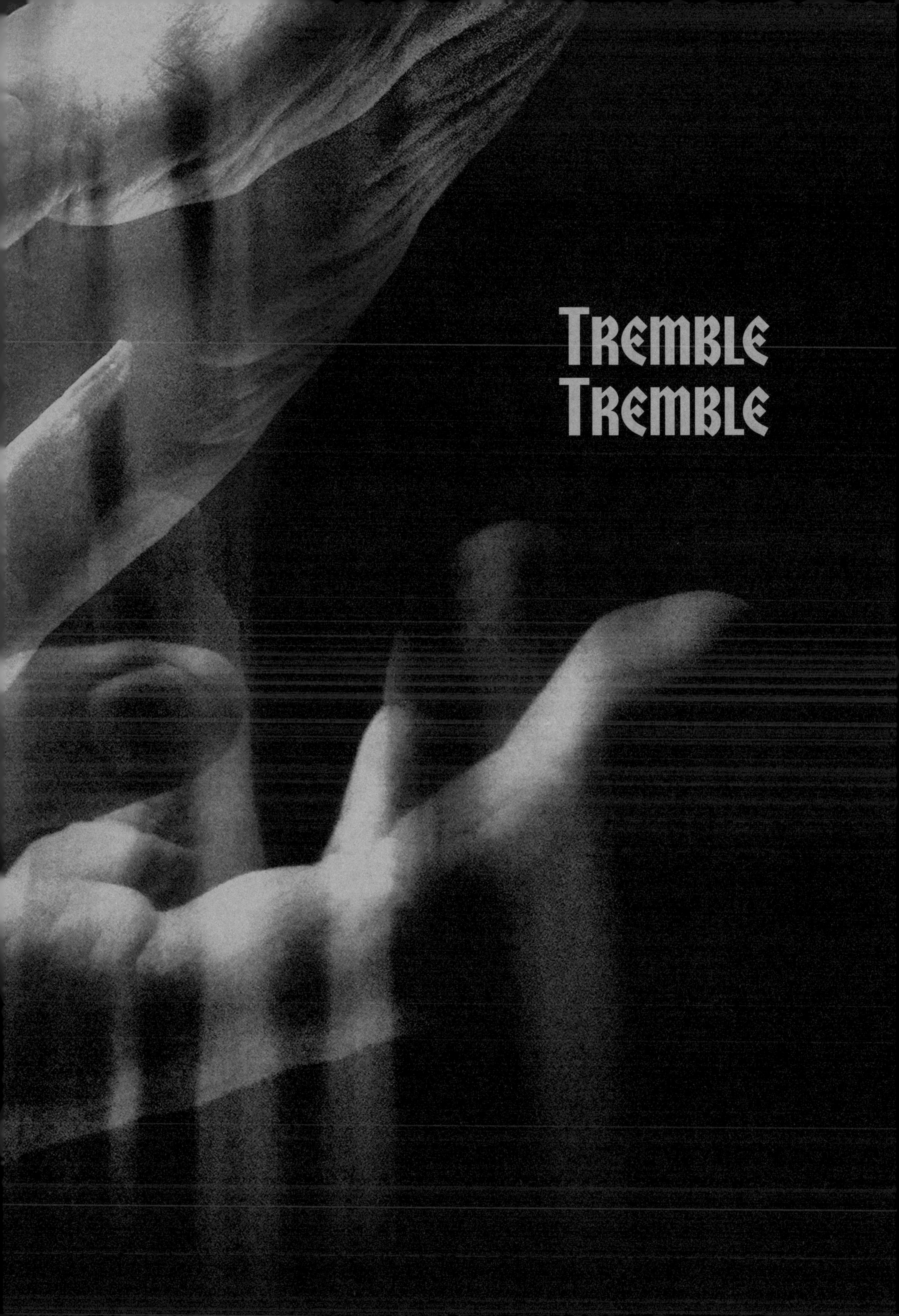

TREMBLE
TREMBLE

(Ireland.)

A

# BILL

To repeal an Act, made in the Parliament of *Ireland*, in the 28th year of the Reign of Queen *Elizabeth*, against Witchcraft and Sorcery.

*Note.—The Figure in the Margin denotes the Number of the Folio in the written Copy.*

Donna Haraway

Since the burning of the first witch in Europe, 800 years ago, 28 generations of women have lived. This giant stretch of time, the knotted entanglement of these women and their histories – from womb to cradle, from oppression to rebellion – runs as a continuous rope through *Tremble Tremble*. Although Jesse Jones' research and curiosity has taken her from courtrooms to parliamentary archives, from feminist workshops to wilderness retreats, *Tremble Tremble* revolves not so much around the evidence of her artistic findings, but around a plausible, ancient truth in which the multitude are brought together in a symbolic, gigantic body, within the law of *In Utera Gigantae*. The artist created this myth, establishing the giant's womb as the site of the only true law. Through scale and bodily form, from the infant to the giant, Jesse Jones' fictional *In Utera Gigantae* suggests that the maternal body supersedes all laws – and proposes a new story of origin for political feminism.

In making an artwork for a National Pavilion in Venice, there's no getting around the fact that the artist is working from a specific place, activating an artwork in what feels much like a temporary cultural embassy, representing the State, on foreign soil. *Tremble Tremble*'s 'witching' of the judicial system is an inversion, turning common law inside out, and imagining an alternative original history for women

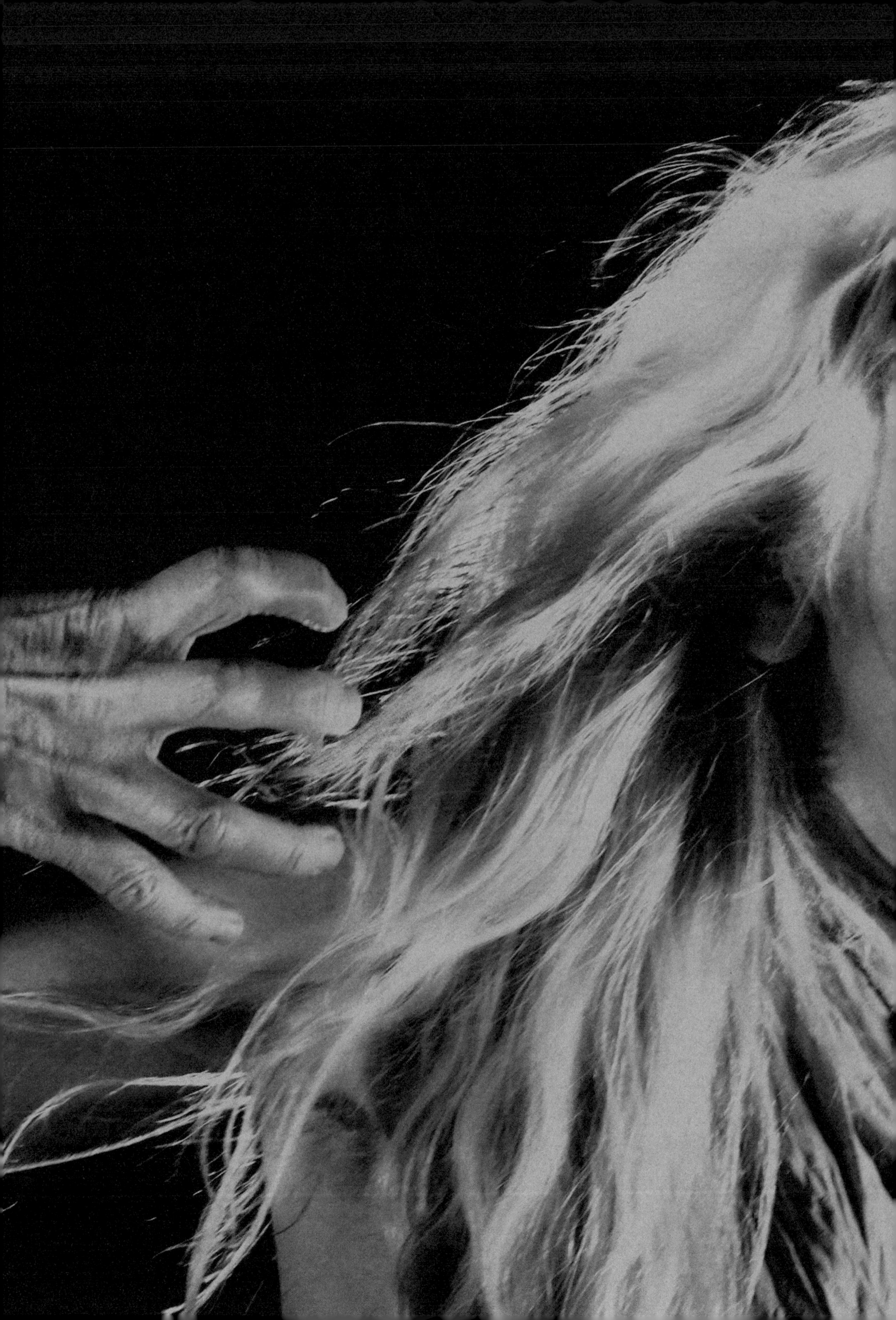

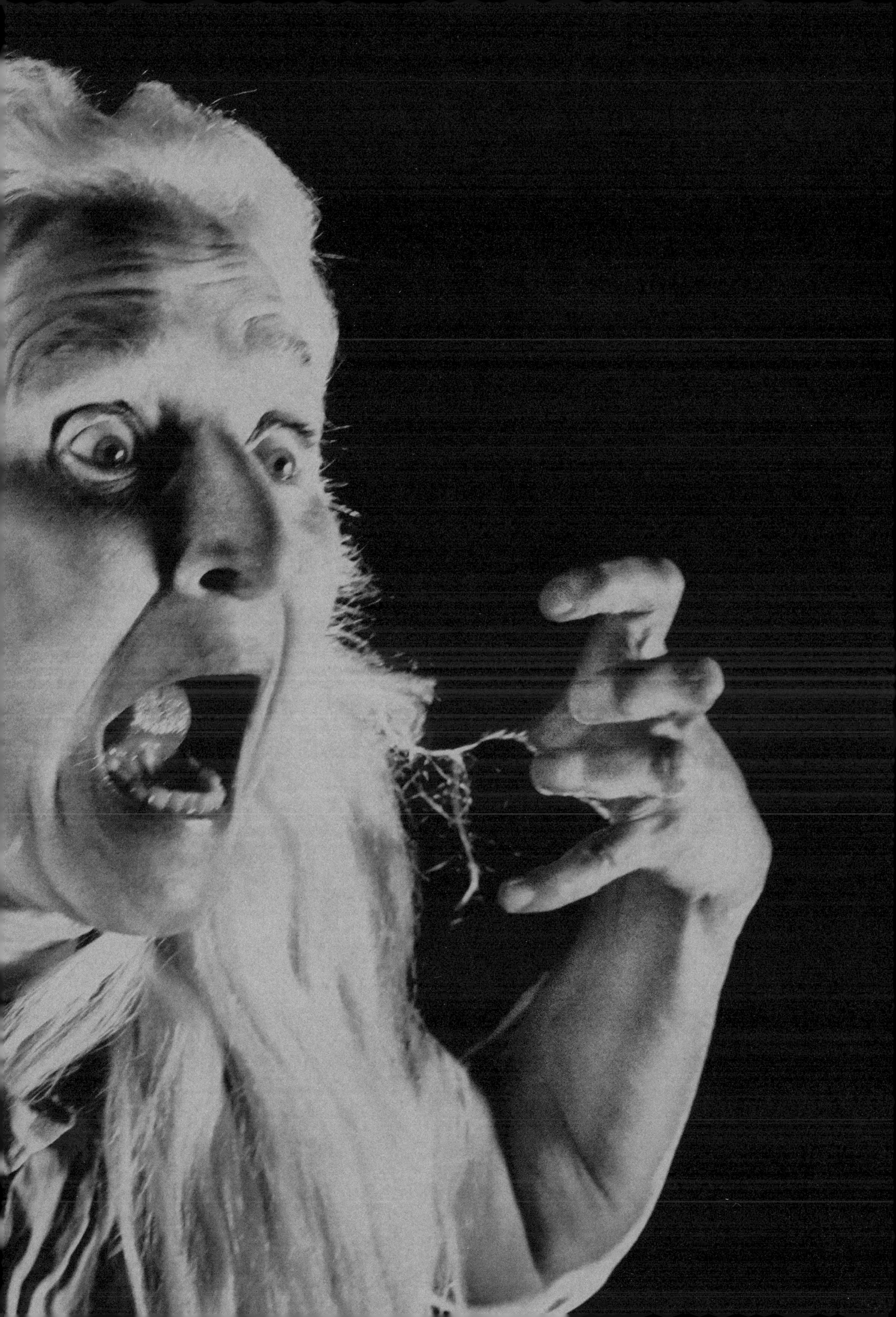

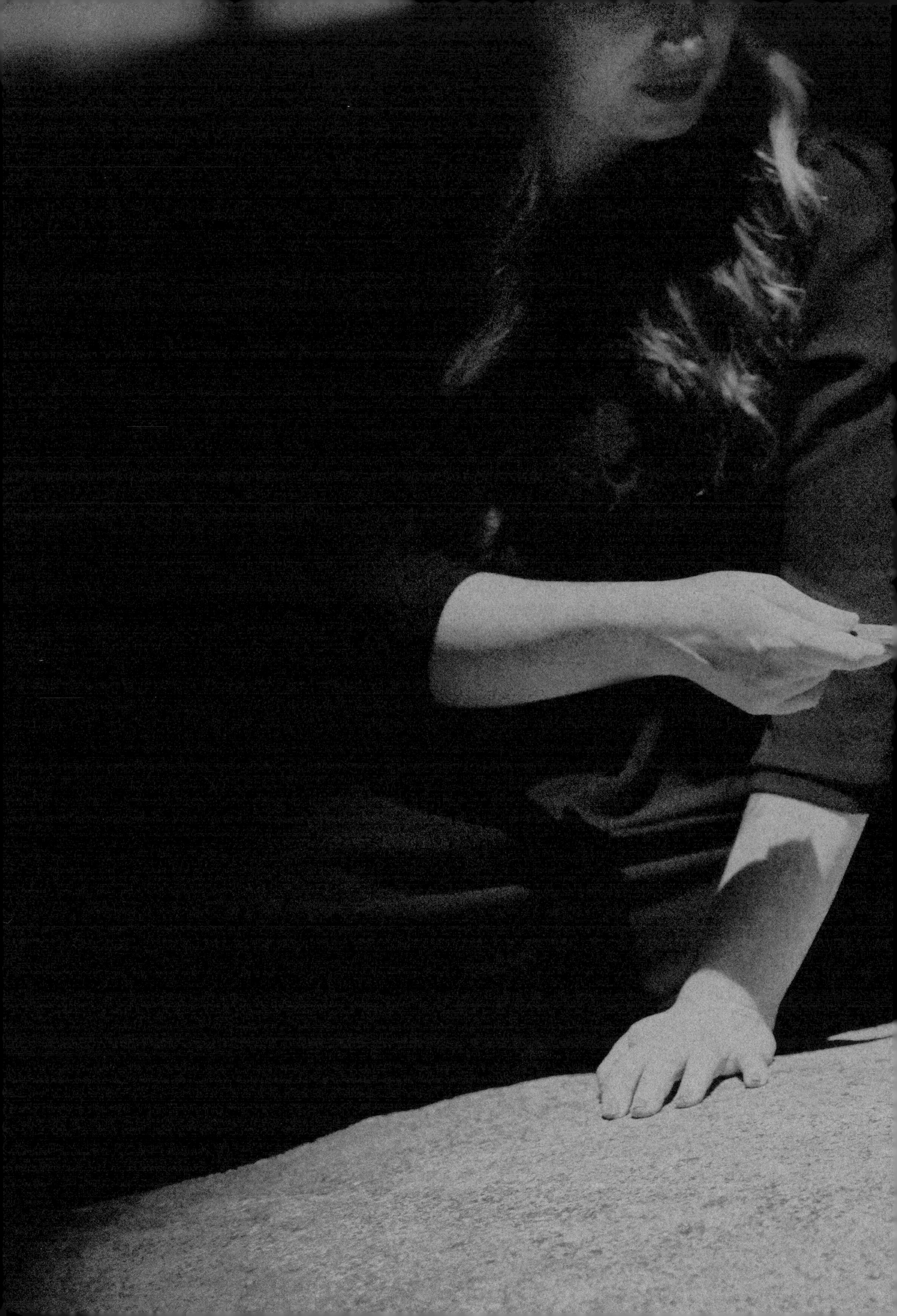

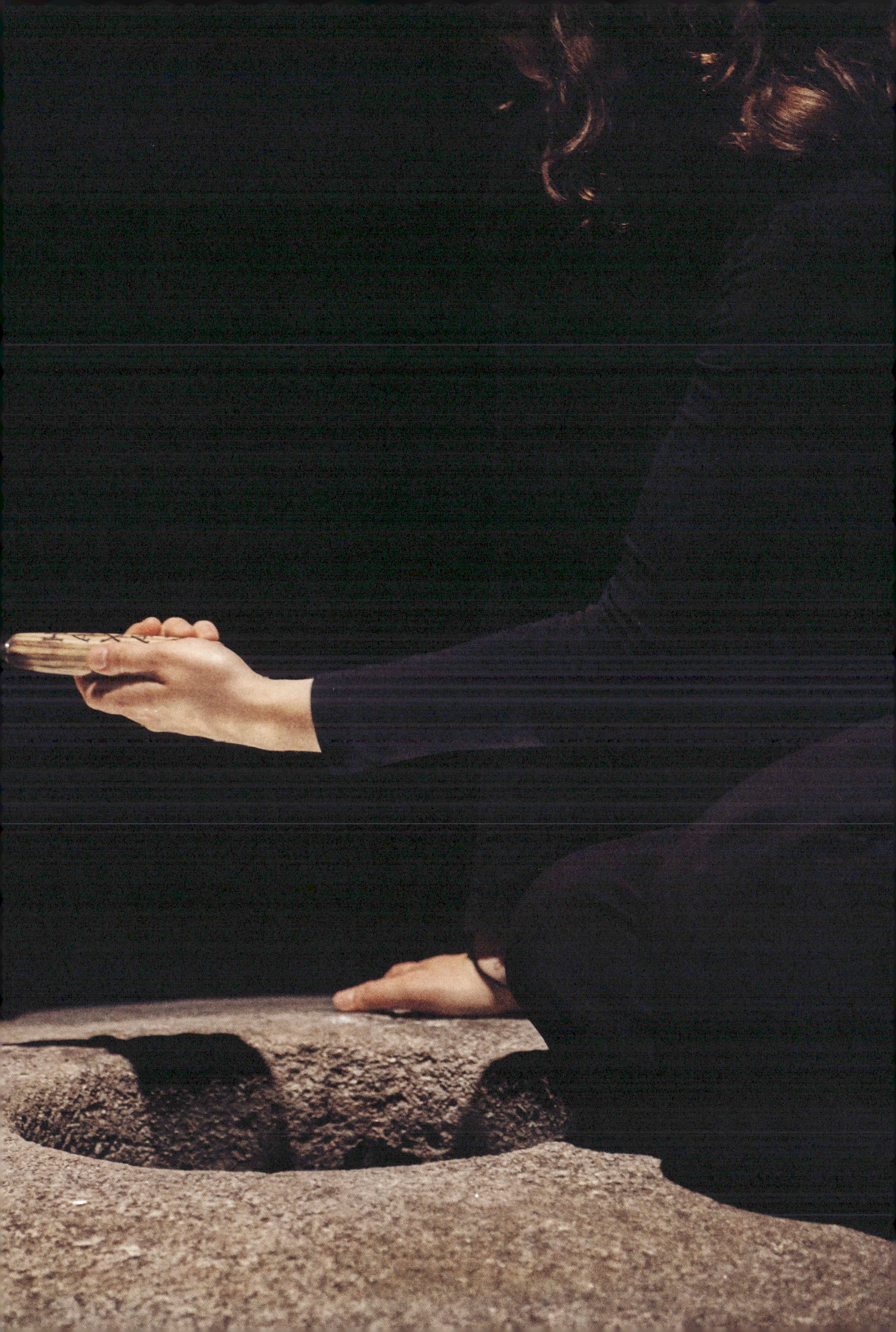

When describing what led to the historical oppression of women succinctly, Silvia Federici writes: 'There is no doubt that in the transition from feudalism to capitalism women suffered a unique process of social degradation that was fundamental to the accumulation of capital and has remained so ever since.'[2]

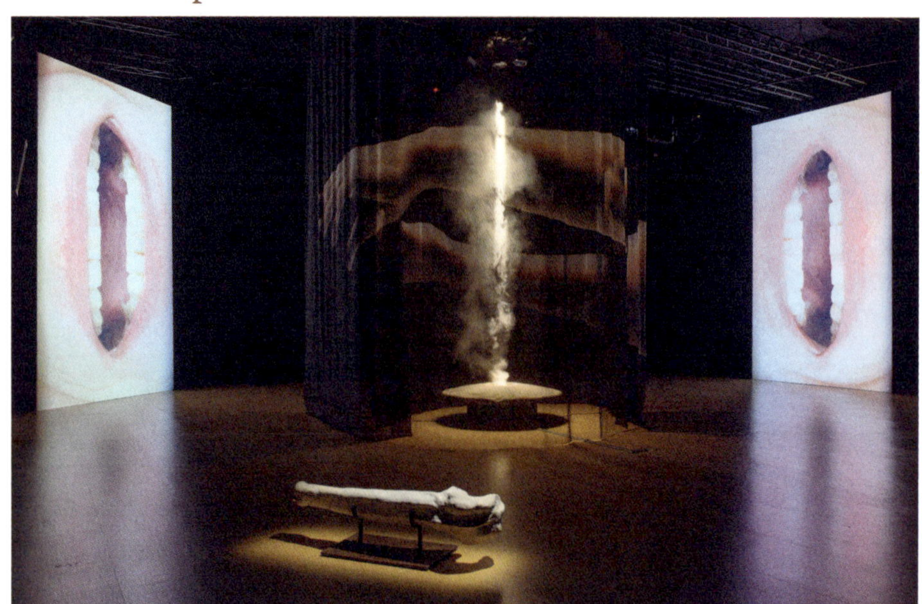

*Tremble Tremble*'s title is inspired by the 1970s Italian 'Wages for Housework' campaign (during which women chanted 'Tremate, tremate, le streghe sono tornate!' – Tremble, tremble, the witches have returned!). Drawing on this movement, Jones conflates the memory of the witch hysteria with the oppression of women and their reduction to the status of unpaid domestic labourer. Within this deeper layer of women's history, it was Jones' determination from the outset to create an alternative site of the State, emerging from the very real social change that had been sweeping Ireland in recent years – a call for the fundamental transformation of the historic relationship between Church and State.[3] Into this time of change in 2017, Jesse Jones restored the witch as a feminist archetype, a disrupter who possesses the potential to transform reality.

This witch, created together by Jesse Jones and the extraordinary performer and artist Olwen Fouéré, drew on many of the women and histories described in the essays in this book. But Jones also owes a great debt of movement to the radical choreographer and dancer Mary Wigman, who both she and Fouéré have studied. Wigman writes of her own practice, of what she calls 'elemental dances':

> [Elemental dances] are the medium and symbol of those forces born of the soil. Their purest form is the demoniacal grotesque in all its variations. Everything apparitional, spectral, whether confined to earthly or released to transcendental experiences is fashioned out of the grotesque. All sensations of anxiety, all chaotic conditions of despair arising from torment, hatred, or fury, grow in this medium of expression up to and beyond the boundaries of the purely human and blend themselves with inhuman, demoniacal violence.[4]

Olwen Fouéré is revered for her adaptation of the voice of the river in James Joyce's *Finnegans Wake*, as well as for countless performances, adaptations and translations for the stage, screen and exhibition contexts. Fouéré collaborated with Jesse Jones throughout the creation of *Tremble Tremble*, and her study of Mary Wigman has informed the increasingly elemental movements of her Giantess, that oscillate between the wildly pounding movements typical of Wigman's *Hexentanz* (1914) and the rock-like permanence of the eternal, and sometimes sleeping, Giantess. The Giantess applies to a concept of time that is outside our current epoch, she lives outside the time of those worldwide stories of origin in which countries and peoples are born of giants. She is geological. Her groaning breath is the breath of rock and her eyes seek us out from an incomprehensible distance. Within her world, we are miniature, vulnerable, nurtured and infected. Her law is the law, not made nor understood by humankind, and her subjects are not answerable to the laws of their peers in power.

Jesse Jones has often employed the dissociative, alienating quality of Brechtian estrangement in re-working historical documents. In *The Spectre and the Sphere* (2007), Jones turned *L'Internationale* into a ghost-tune, having it performed as a theremin-enchantment in an old socialist building turned arts centre. In *The Other North* (2013), she took a conflict resolution therapy session held in the early 1970s by American psychologist

Carl Rogers in Northern Ireland, and restaged it as a re-enactment script for Korean protagonists. Creating a direct association between the Republic of Ireland/Northern Ireland, and South Korea/North Korea, *The Other North* made the othering effect of inhabiting foreign words and positions (as actors, agents and citizens) the real political basis of the work. In the 2016 work, *The Touching Contract* (made with artist Sarah Browne) commissioned by Artangel, Jones took first-hand accounts of legal violations, bodily submission to authority, and transformed them into a physical, political encounter with touch through an immersive, live performance. The performer's contact with members of the audience ranged from oppressive and challenging to tender and moving. Jones' research oscillates from forensic to idiosyncratic, but the abstraction of the final artworks, indicates that Jones is deeply distrustful of the shape of evidence.

Although Jones has studied the evidentiary role of objects and the law at length, particularly in relation to Ireland's symphysiotomy trials, the sculptural objects encountered in the installation of *Tremble Tremble* are of a much more speculative origin. Pursuing a long-term archaeology of a collective unconscious, Jones connects her mythological giant (born of Celtic origin stories) to the 3.18 million-year-old skeletal specimen Lucy the *Australopithecus* (a hominid species who predates Homo erectus, Homo sapien and Neanderthal), and the oldest known specimen in the world. The white, bone-shaped sculptures are giant-sized 'evidence' of the speculative pre-history from which the law of *In Utera Gigantae* is said to have originated, and it is Lucy's story that Olwen Fouéré recounts as the camera traverses her body as though she is a sleeping-giant landscape.

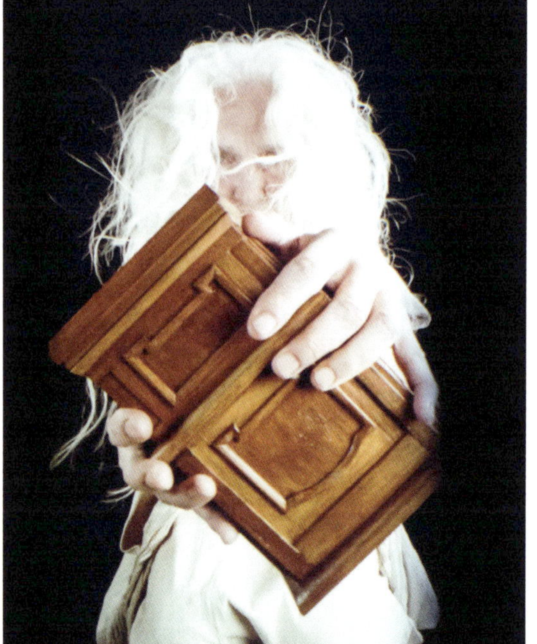

On screen, authentic courthouse and church remnants also appear as relics of the past (or some incomprehensible future). Amputated from their context and authority, they float in a blackened wasteland. The residual power of these objects is by turns explored, dismantled and overturned, with an unfamiliar air of curiosity. This evidence is something between totem and detritus, describing more about the social order of the people who built it than any kind of inference of power or authority.

Yet, inside all raw materials there lies a sort of consciousness, an expression of matter born of time, pressure, heat and growth. The natural authority of wood can be traced from the authority of kings to that of the courts. Long before courthouses were made, full of ornate wooden panelling, impressive angular boxes and individually decorated pews, kings and leaders would speak before a commanding tree. Not only did the reverence for the natural world and her many wonders infer power and immutability, but the raw material also provided natural amplification for the speaker, allowing the voice to be carried, and obeyed. The weight of the former courthouse in *Tremble Tremble* is immense – the old, dead weight you find in very dense wood – and its surface is mottled and aged. This material still retains its memory of authority, even in its fractured state. It has been a silent witness to lives, offences, lies, justice, despair, brutality, forgiveness, corruption, wisdom, love and injustice. While all things have the potential to accrue aura, Jesse Jones' commandeering of this judicial artefact suggests an overturning of the historical power and dominion of the courts. As the Giantess in the two towering screens dwarfs the courthouse relic and eventually cradles it in her hand, the usurping of power is almost farcical in its crushing imbalance of size and weight, careful as she is not to damage humankind's artefact. This delicate wooden object is clearly not the history of the Giantess, but it *is* history.

Again distrustful of the shape of evidence, Jones presents text taken from that most insidious of tomes – the guidebook to the persecution of witches. In *Tremble Tremble* the *Malleus Maleficarum* (1487) is garbled and reversed by Fouéré: undone, invalidated, repealed. Commonly known as the *Hammer of Witches*, the *Malleus Maleficarum* was essentially a guide to identifying, accusing, trying and destroying women accused of witchcraft, which sold more copies than any other book except the Bible until 1678.

Testimonies from women who have challenged, become entangled, or instigated change in the law around women's rights are worked into various passages. The scene in which the Giantess looms over us begins with testimony from Temperance Lloyd,

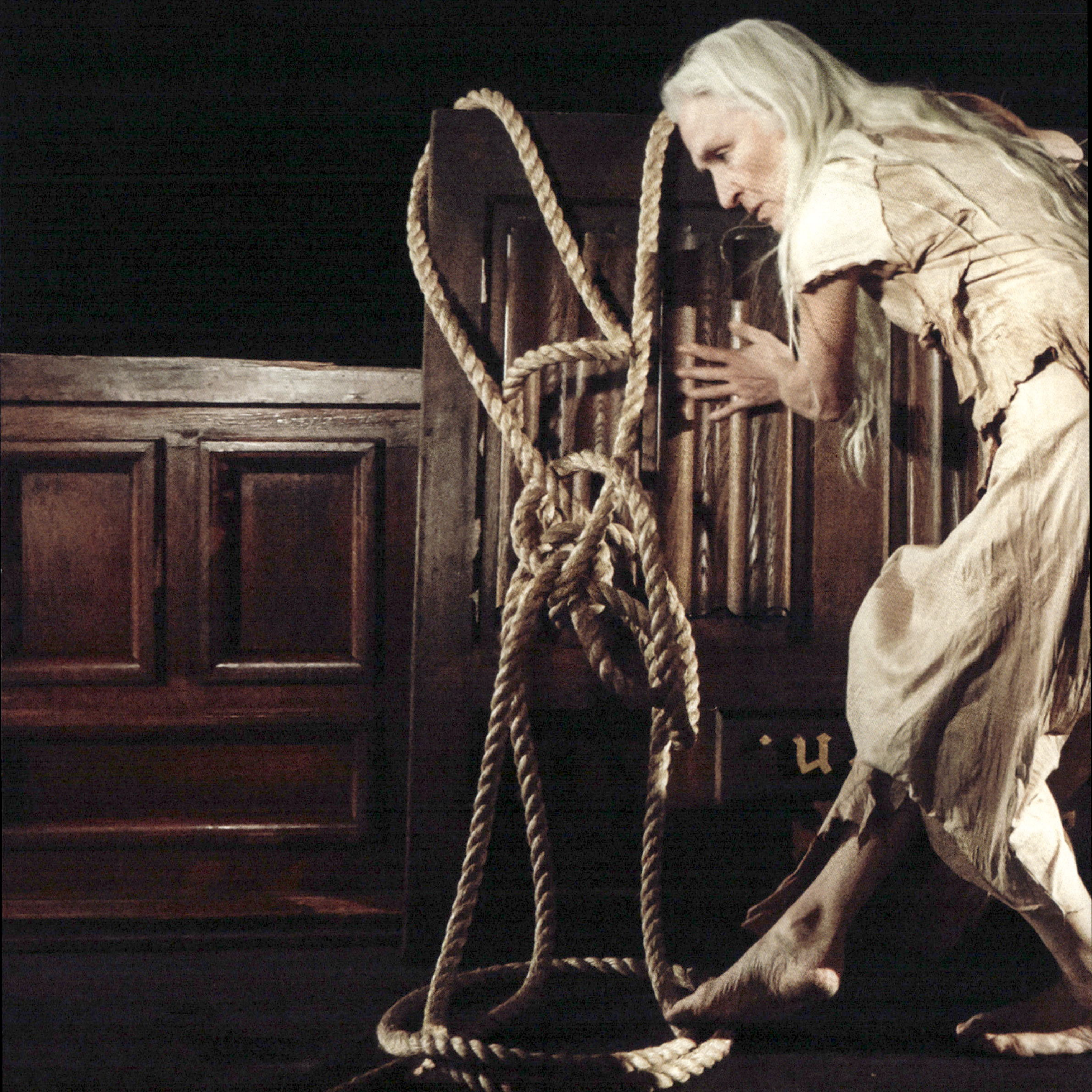

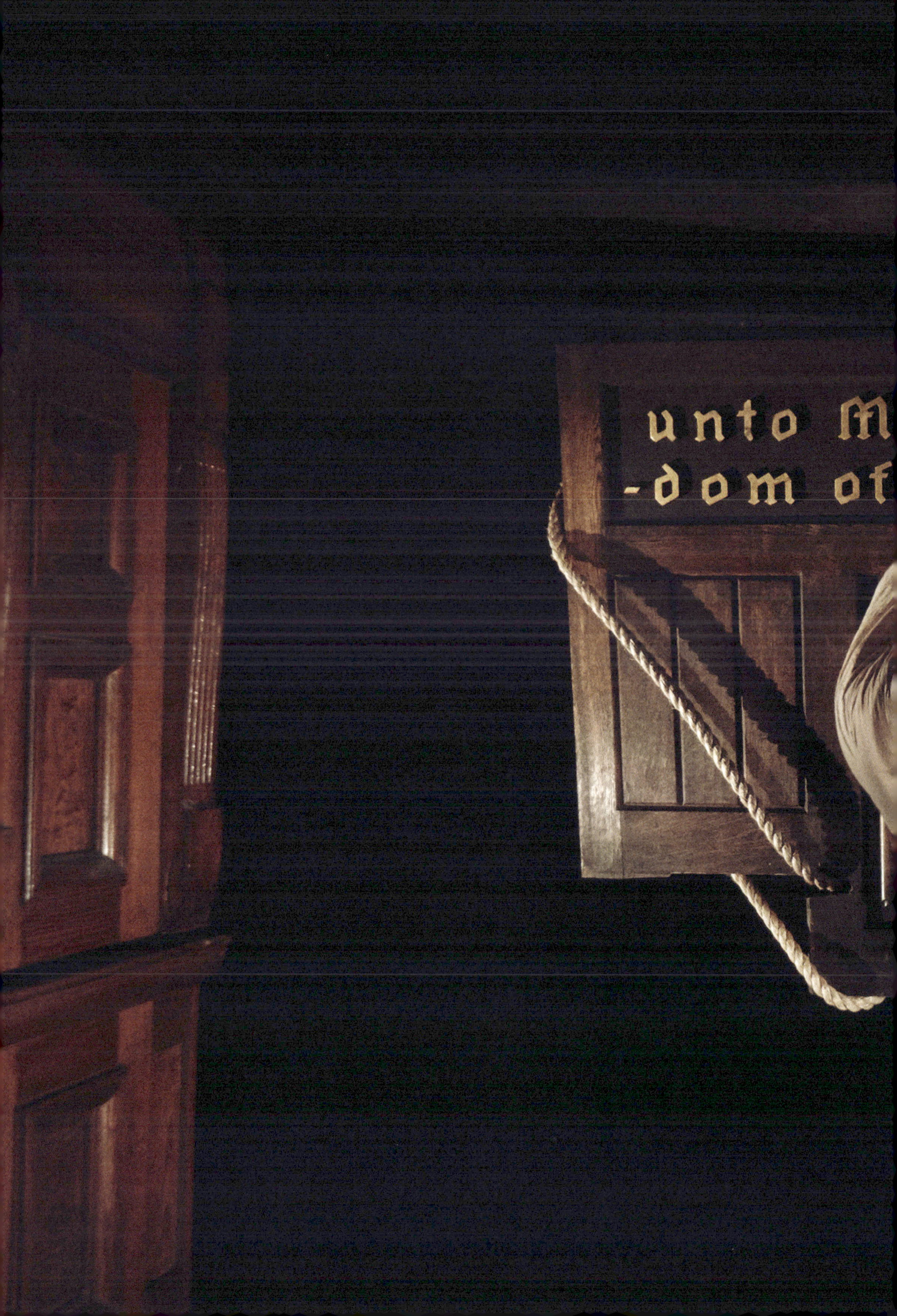

unto M
-dom of

accused of witchcraft and burned at the stake in the town of Bideford, Devon, UK in 1682: 'Did I disturb ye good people? I hopes I disturb ye, I hopes I disturb ye enough to want to see this, your house, in ruins all around ye! Have you had enough yet? Or do you still have time for chaos? Hah? More?' Also evoked are Simone Veil (the French Minister for Health who almost single-handedly pushed forward the law legalising abortion in France in 1975), and Henrietta Lacks, whose rapidly multiplying cells were sampled without her consent and became the basis of the immortal HeLa cell line. (Lacks' family were not informed of this cellular legacy, only finding out about the harvesting and

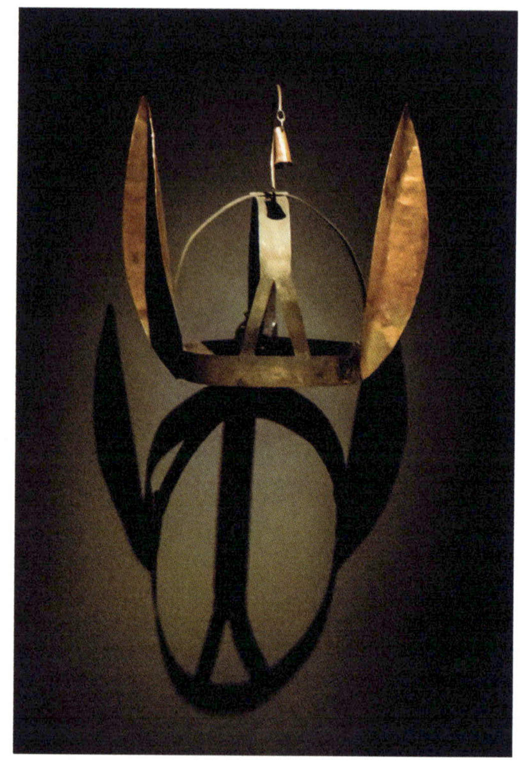

subsequent distribution of her bodily material throughout the world for medical advancement decades after Henrietta's death.)

When showing the work in Scotland at Talbot Rice Gallery, Jones included a newly made 'scold's bridle'. These were intended to muzzle a woman accused of witchcraft and silence the power of her speech. Many scold's bridles were decorated or made to reference animal forms, as women were paraded through Scottish villages and towns as a public shaming, inducing terror. Jones states, 'with *Tremble Tremble* I wanted to make something that wasn't just a representation of the story of feminism, or the return of witch-power, I wanted to make [an artwork] that incorporated some of the physical and material apparatus of witchcraft … Some aspects of the artwork have been communicated to me through tarot cards or come together through processes of dreaming. It's deeply connected to my unconscious, as well as my research and political and rational consciousness. People feel very confused with [the current] break between truth and language … how do we merge the cerebral and the intellectual with what we might *feel* politically?'

The thirty-minute experience of *Tremble Tremble* is indicative of what Jones calls 'expanded cinema', where objects are arranged 'like runes'. Large-scale curtains that contain images of enveloping arms were pulled through the space by performers, and a circle was ritualistically carved into the wall throughout the day. It was restaged for the particular spaces in which it is shown: the Arsenale in the Venice Biennale; a huge white cube at LASALLE College of the Arts in Singapore; a black-box theatre at Project Arts Centre in Dublin; a neo-classical Georgian gallery at Talbot Rice Gallery in Edinburgh; a transformed gallery of Museo Guggenheim in Bilbao; or SAMSTAG's voluminous galleries in the context of Adelaide Festival. Connecting to local histories and tracing the historical oppression of women and communities around the world, new elements were developed as the work travelled: in Dublin, the performers used a brass tap to drink water from the holy

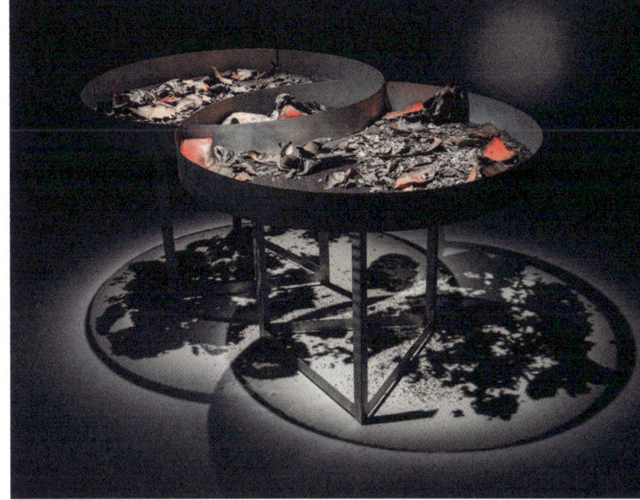

wells of St Brigid, collected by anthropologist Sara O'Rourke, and infused with a herbal spell made by Idle Women from Pendle (Quench thy Thirst, but not thy Rage); in Singapore, an Irish declaration from 1821 repealing the Witchcraft Act of 1586 (that had been quietly on display at every venue) was burned on a table in the tradition of the Hungry Ghost, effectively sending the ancestors (or medieval Irish women) the tools for their emancipation. Other tools entered the artwork – hammers inscribed with 'Thou Shalt Not Suffer' were created, based on the original art-tool hammers of Father Joseph McNally, founder of LASALLE College of the Arts, and missionary brother, teacher and sculptor.[5] In Bilbao, Jones expanded this hybrid archive with talismanic material from another Catholic priest: an owl's head used to ward off malefi-

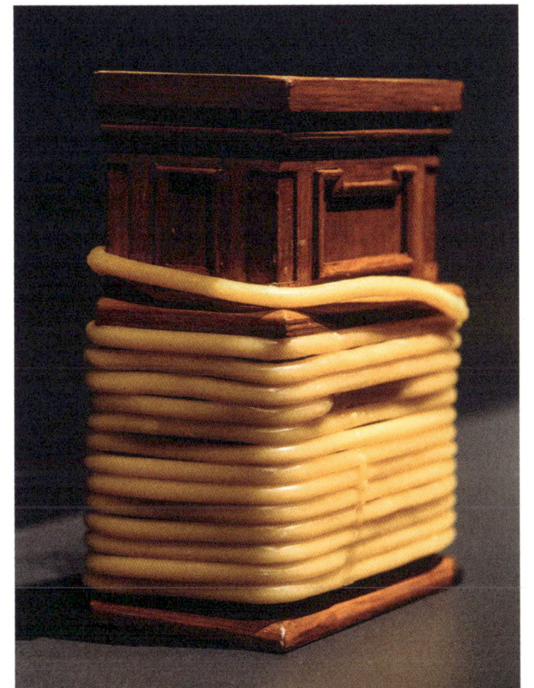

cence was placed at the entrance of the Museo Guggenheim's gallery, dimly lit in the dark. Also in Bilbao, Jones created new sculptures based on the Basque wax tablets called *argizaiola*, designed to ward off nefarious spirits (burned on the opening night of the exhibition); and further to the scold's bridle, in Edinburgh, Jones fashioned what appeared to be a new gaping crack in the ancient floorboards of the

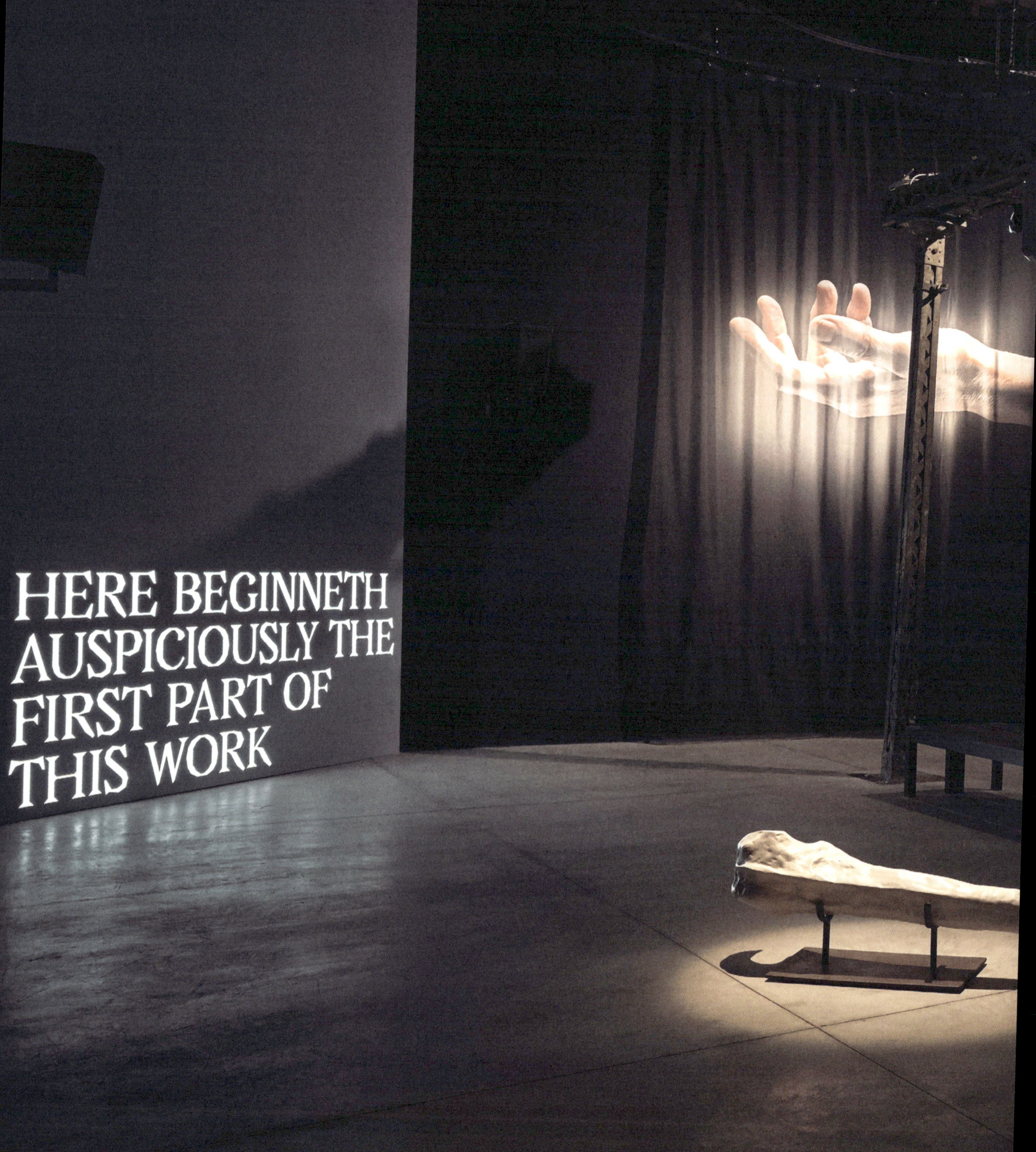

HERE BEGINNETH
AUSPICIOUSLY THE
FIRST PART OF
THIS WORK

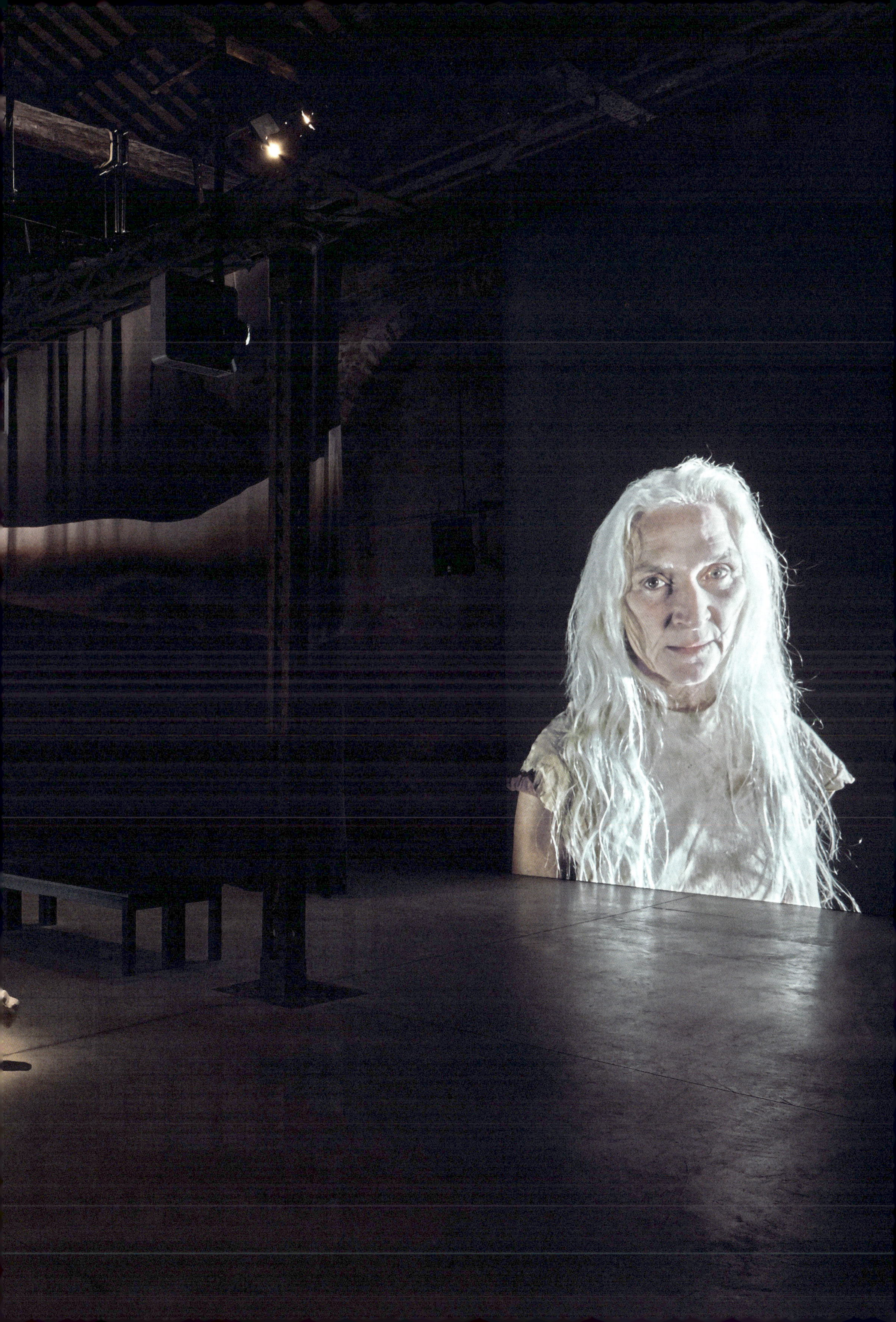

former Natural History Museum, William Henry Playfair's decorative Georgian Gallery. Plumes of smoke emerged from the crack (carved in the likeness of the chasm over which would wait the Oracle of Delphi), and from the heart of Edinburgh's patriarchal history, implying a female seer had been made manifest within the University's Old College.

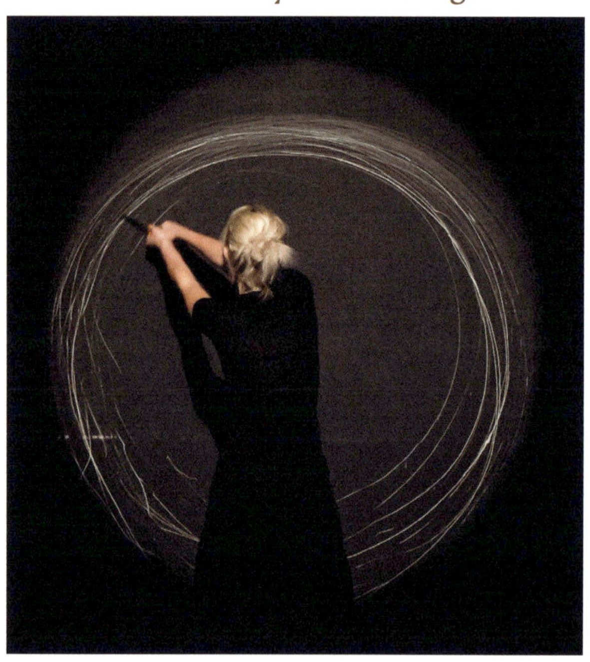

Underlying *Tremble Tremble* is also the unknown woman, or group of women, who made the curious and enigmatic marks on the ancient Ishango bone. Discovered in 1960 in Central Africa, the bone was originally thought to be 5,000 years old, and its methodical and deliberate markings were attributed to the birth of mathematics, varying from single marks, to clusters of 3 or 5, to larger, more regular clusters of 19 and 22. Microscopic study and further perspectives have since aged this baboon fibula bone at 25,000 years old, and presented the argument that the Ishango bone's markings are more likely to be evidence of female wisdom and a commune with the lunar cycle, than mathematical advancement. So, was this stick, the famous and treasured Ishango bone, a stone-age fertility tracker? As Donna Haraway writes: 'One important route for reconstructing socialist-feminist politics is through theory and practice addressed to the social relations of science and technology, including crucially the systems of myth and meanings structuring our imaginations.'[6]

Thrumming, beating and trilling throughout *Tremble Tremble* is a sound score composed by Susan Stenger, a sound artist who composes with drones and layers, with simple, rhythmic and melodic structures, creating what she calls 'sonic reactions'. Although Stenger took the markings of the Ishango bone as the basis for a graphic score, its rhythms and beats have detached from their origin, now composed and installed specifically for the various sites of *Tremble Tremble*.

The haunting lyrics written by Jones as the work song of the Giantess are set to a melody by Stenger. Informed by historical work songs, the droning, repetitive, catchy melody was performed by Olwen Fouéré:

I HAD A NAME THAT I'VE FORGOTTEN
THEY CALL ME DOG WOMAN – IT WILL DO
I'LL PUSH AND PULL AND TURN THIS COURTHOUSE TO CINDERS
BY A BLOOD FULL MOON
I WILL WEAVE YOUR ROPE TO SATIN
AND WITCH THE HARVEST THAT YOU SOW
ALL THAT IS, HAS ITS OTHER
AS ABOVE
SHALL BE BELOW
ALL THAT IS, HAS ITS OTHER
AS ABOVE
SHALL BE BELOW
I'LL DRINK YOUR WINE AND SPOIL THE BARRELS
YOUR HOUSE IN RUINS AT MY FEET
MY BROKEN BONES SHALL BE A WEAPON
CHAOS IS THE BREAD I EAT
MY BROKEN BONES SHALL BE A WEAPON
CHAOS IS THE BREAD I EAT
REJECT THE LAW THAT ALL MEN FOLLOW
YIELD TO WHAT YOU CANNOT KNOW
ALL YOUR TRIALS SHALL BE FORGOTTEN
AS ABOVE
SHALL BE BELOW
NO TO LAW THAT ALL MEN FOLLOW
YES TO WHAT YOU CANNOT KNOW
ALL YOUR TRIALS SHALL BE FORGOTTEN
AS ABOVE
SHALL BE BELOW

*Dog Woman's Song*

To this tune, Jones' work lifts its foot into the air and stomps down with purpose.

Tremate, Tremate.

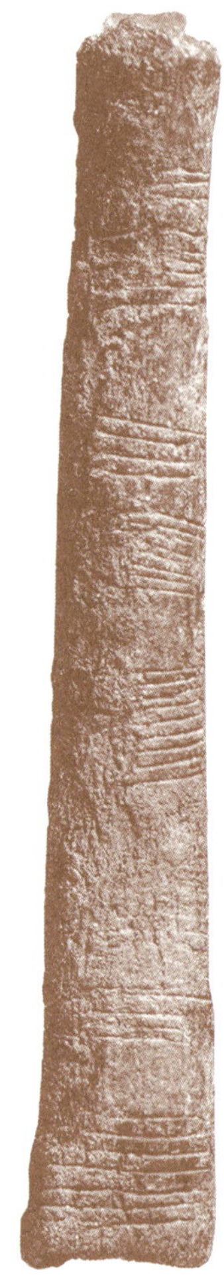


1.

Haraway, D. (2003) 'A Cyborg Manifesto', *The Feminism and Visual Culture Reader*, Jones, A. (ed), London and New York, Routledge, p. 481. Originally published in Haraway, D. (1991) *Simians, Cyborgs, and Women: The Reinvention of Nature*, London, Free Association Books.

2.

Federici, S. (2014 [2004]) *Caliban and the Witch*, Brooklyn, New York, Autonomedia, p. 75.

3.

See *Did We Disturb You Good People?*, on p. 61 of this publication.

4.

From Walter Sorell's translation of Mary Wigman's writings cited by Barbara Hales. 'Mediating Worlds: The Occult as Projection of the New Woman in Weimar Culture' (2010), *The German Quarterly*, American Association of Teachers of German, New Jersey, Wiley-Blackwell, vol. 83, no. 3, p. 323.

5.

An edition of *Thou Shalt Not Suffer* (2018) is currently held in the collection of Edinburgh University.

6.

Haraway, D. 'A Cyborg Manifesto', p. 485.


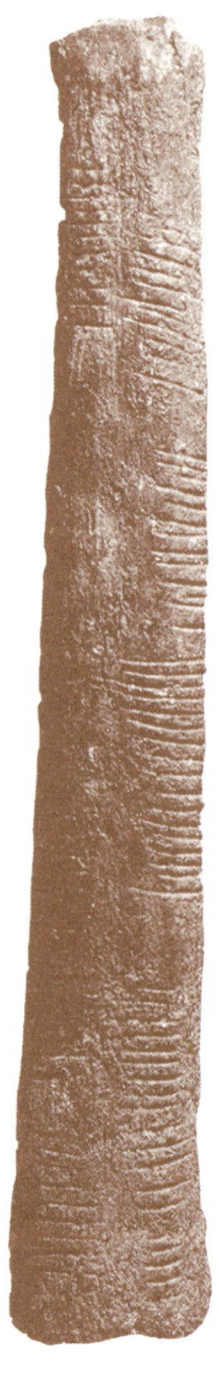

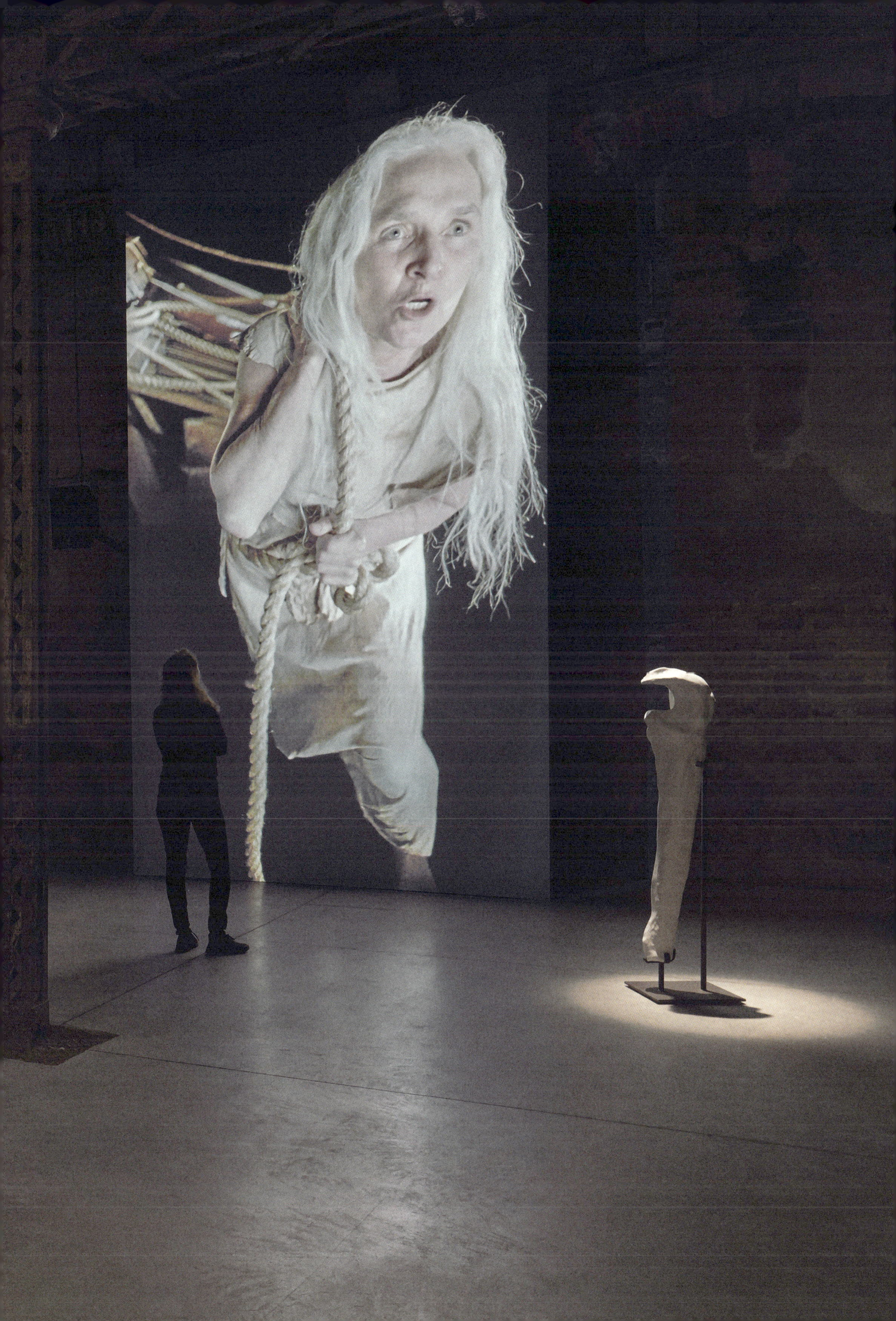

# In Praise of the Dancing Body

Silvia Federici

The history of the body is the history of human beings, for there is no cultural practice that is not first applied to the body. Even if we limit ourselves to speak of the history of the body in capitalism we face an overwhelming task, so extensive have been the techniques used to discipline the body, constantly changing, depending on the shifts in labour regimes to which our body was subjected to. Moreover, we do not have one history but different histories of the body: the body of men, of women, of the waged worker, of the enslaved, of the colonised.

A history of the body then can be reconstructed by describing the different forms of repression that capitalism has activated against it. But I have decided to speak instead of the body as a ground of resistance, that is, the body and its powers – the power to act, to transform itself and the world, and the body as a natural limit to exploitation.

There is something we have lost in our insistence on the body as something socially constructed and performative. The view of the body as a social [discursive] production has hidden the fact that our body is a receptacle of powers, capacities and resistances, that have been developed in a long process of co-evolution with our natural environment, as well as intergenerational practices that have made it a natural limit to exploitation.

By the body as a 'natural limit' I refer to the structure of needs and desires created in us not only by our conscious decisions or collective practices, but by millions of years of material evolution: the need for the sun, for the blue sky and the green of trees, for the smell of the woods and the oceans, the need for touching, smelling, sleeping, making love.

This accumulated structure of needs and desires, that for thousands of years have been the condition of our social reproduction, has put limits to our exploitation, and is something that capitalism has incessantly struggled to overcome.

Capitalism was not the first system based on the exploitation of human labour. But more than any other system in history, it has tried to create an economic world where labour is the most essential principle of accumulation. As such it was the first to make the regimentation and mechanisation of the body a key premise of the accumulation of wealth. Indeed, one of capitalism's main social tasks from its beginning to the present has been the transformation of our energies and corporeal powers into labour powers.

In *Caliban and the Witch* (2004), I have looked at the strategies that capitalism has employed to accomplish this task and remould human nature, in the same way as it has tried to remould the earth in order to make the land more productive and to turn animals into living factories. I have spoken of the historic battle it has waged against the body, against our materiality, and the many institutions it has created for this purpose: the law, the whip, the regulation of sexuality, as well as a myriad of social practices that have redefined our relation to space, to nature and to each other.

Capitalism was born from the separation of people from the land. Its first task was to make work independent of the seasons and to lengthen the workday beyond the limits of our endurance. Generally, we stress the economic aspect of this process, the economic dependence capitalism has created on monetary relations, and its role in the formation of a wage proletariat. What we have not always seen is what the separation from the land and nature has meant for our body, which has been pauperised and stripped of the powers that pre-capitalist populations attributed to it.

Nature is our inorganic body and there was a time when we could read the winds, the clouds, and the changes in the currents of rivers and seas. In pre-capitalist societies, people thought they had the power to fly, to have out-of-body experiences, to communicate, to speak with animals and take on their powers, and even shape-shift. They also thought that they could be in more places than one and, for example, they could come back from the grave to take revenge on their enemies.

Not all these powers were imaginary. Daily contact with nature was the source of a great amount of knowledge, reflected in the food revolution that took place especially in the Americas prior to colonisation, or in the revolution in sailing techniques. We know now, for instance, that the Polynesian populations used to travel the high seas at night with only their body as their compass, as they could tell from the vibrations of the waves the different ways to direct their boats to the shore.

Fixation in space and time has been one of the most elementary and persistent techniques capitalism has used to take hold of the body – see the attacks throughout history on vagabonds, migrants, hobo-men. Mobility is a threat when not pursued for work's sake as it circulates knowledges, experiences, struggles. In the past, the instruments of restraint were whips, chains, the stocks, mutilation, enslavement. Today, in addition to the whip and the detention centres, we have computer surveillance and the periodic threat of epidemics as a means to control nomadism.

Mechanisation, the turning of the body – male and female – into a machine, has been one of capitalism's most relentless pursuits. Animals too are turned into machines, so that sows can double their litter, chickens can produce uninterrupted flows of eggs, while unproductive ones are ground like stones, and calves can never stand on their feet before being brought to the slaughterhouse.

I cannot here evoke all the ways in which the mechanisation of the body has occurred. Enough to say that the techniques of capture and domination have changed depending on the dominant labour regime and the machines that have been the model for the body.

Thus we find that in the sixteenth and seventeenth centuries (the time of manufacture), the body was imagined and disciplined according to the model of simple machines, like the pump and the lever. This was the regime that culminated in Taylorism, time-motion study, where every motion was calculated and all our energies were channelled to the task. Resistance here was imagined in the form of *inertia*, with the body pictured as a dumb animal, a monster resistant to command.

With the nineteenth century we have, instead, a conception of the body and disciplinary techniques modelled on the steam

gime, its productivity calculated in terms of input and output
with efficiency becoming the key word. Under this regime, the
disciplining of the body was accomplished through dietary
restrictions and the calculation of the calories that a working
body would need. The climax, in this context, was the Nazi table
that specified what calories each type of worker needed. The
enemy here was the dispersion of energy, entropy, waste, disorder
In the **US**, the history of this new political economy began in the
1880s, with the attack on the saloon and the remoulding of the
family life with, at its centre, the full-time housewife, conceived
as an anti-entropic device, always on call, ready to restore the
meal consumed, the body sullied after the bath, the dress repaired
and torn again.

In our time, models for the body are the computer and the
genetic code, crafting a dematerialised, disaggregated body
imagined as a conglomerate of cells and genes each with her own
programme, indifferent to the rest and to the good of the body as
a whole. Such is the theory of the *selfish gene*, the idea, that is, that
the body is made of individualistic cells and genes all pursuing
their programme – a perfect metaphor for the neo-liberal conception of life, where market dominance turns
against not only group solidarity but solidarity
with our own selves. Consistently, the body disin-
tegrates into an assemblage of selfish genes, each
striving to achieve its selfish goals, indifferent to
the interest of the rest.

To the extent that we internalise this view,
we internalise the most profound experience of
self-alienation, as we confront not only a great beast that does
not obey our orders, but a host of micro-enemies that are planted
right into our own body, ready to attack us at any moment.
Industries have been built on the fears that this conception of
the body generates, putting us at the mercy of forces that we do
not control. Inevitably, if we internalise this view, we do not taste
good to ourselves. In fact, our body scares us, and we do not listen
to it. We do not hear what it wants, but join the assault on it with
all the weapons that medicine can offer: radiation, colonoscopy,
mammography, all arms in a long battle against the body, with us
joining in the assault rather than taking our body out of the line

of fire. In this way we are prepared to accept a world that transforms body parts into commodities for a market and view our body as a repository of diseases: the body as plague, the body as source of epidemics, the body without reason.

Our struggle then must begin with the reappropriation of our body, the revaluation and rediscovery of its capacity for resistance, and expansion and celebration of its powers, individual and collective.

Dance is central to this reappropriation. In essence, the act of dancing is an exploration and invention of what a body can do: of its capacities, its languages, its articulations of the strivings of our being. I have come to believe that there is a philosophy in dancing, for dance mimics the processes by which we relate to the world, connect with other bodies, transform ourselves and the space around us.

From dance we learn that matter is not stupid, it is not blind, it is not mechanical, but has its rhythms, has its language, and it is self-activated and self-organising. Our bodies have reasons that we need to learn, rediscover, reinvent. We need to listen to their language as the path to our health and healing, as we need to listen to the language and rhythms of the natural world as the path to the health and healing of the earth. Since the power to be affected and to affect, to be moved and move, a capacity which is indestructible, exhausted only with death, is constitutive of the body, there is an immanent politics residing in it: the capacity to transform itself, others, and change the world.

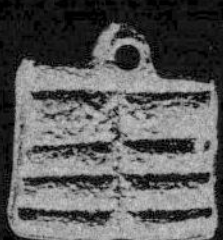

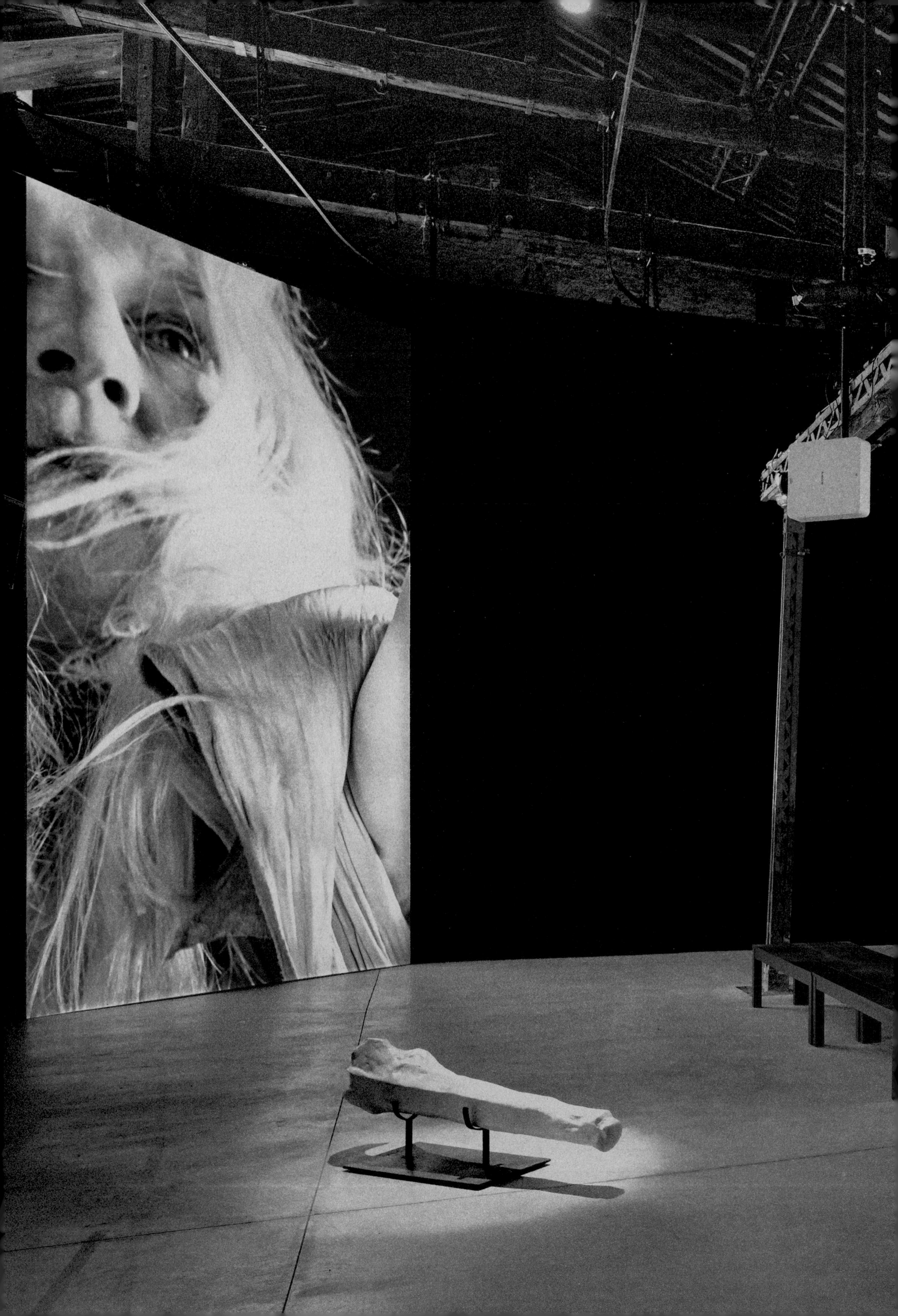

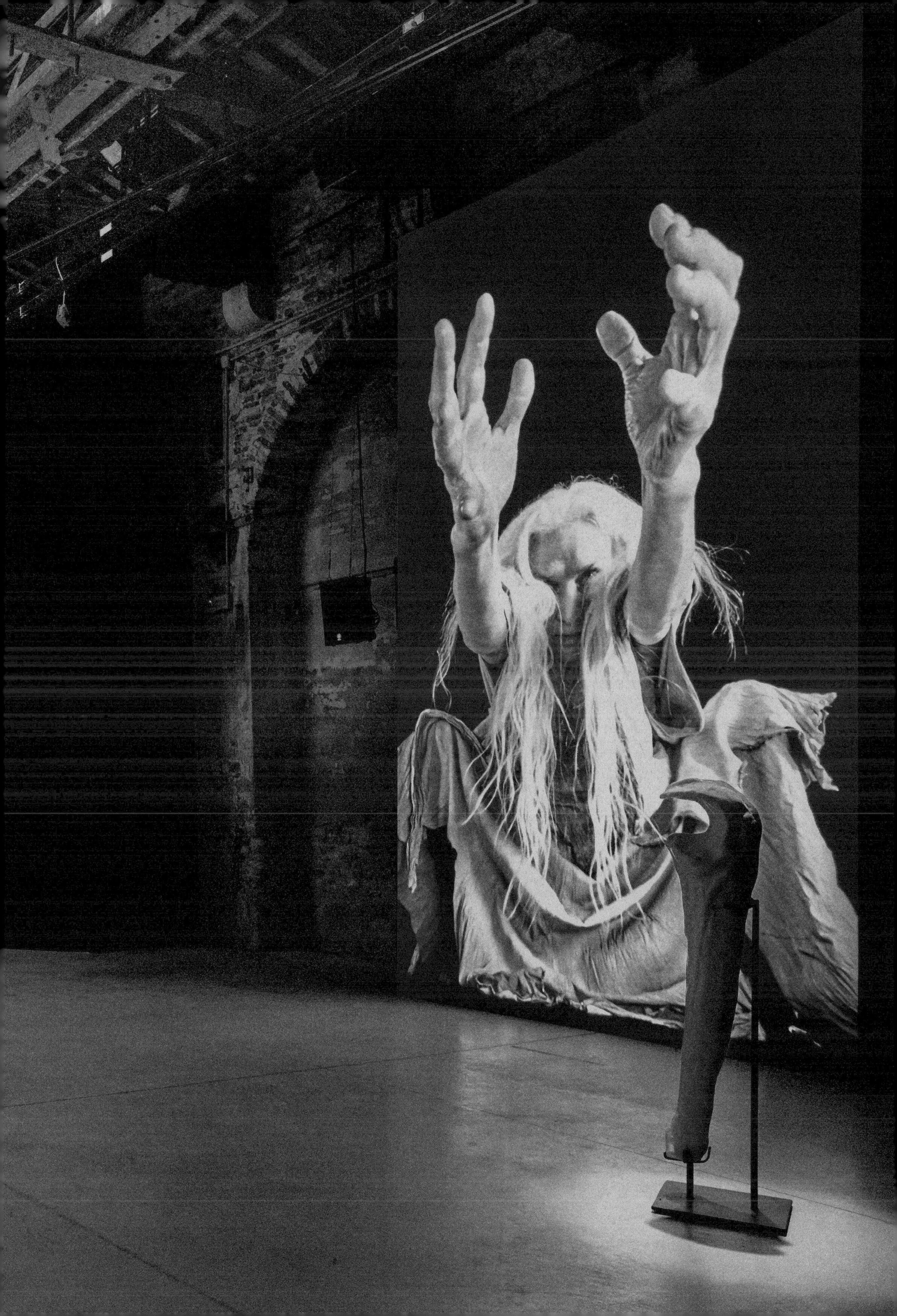

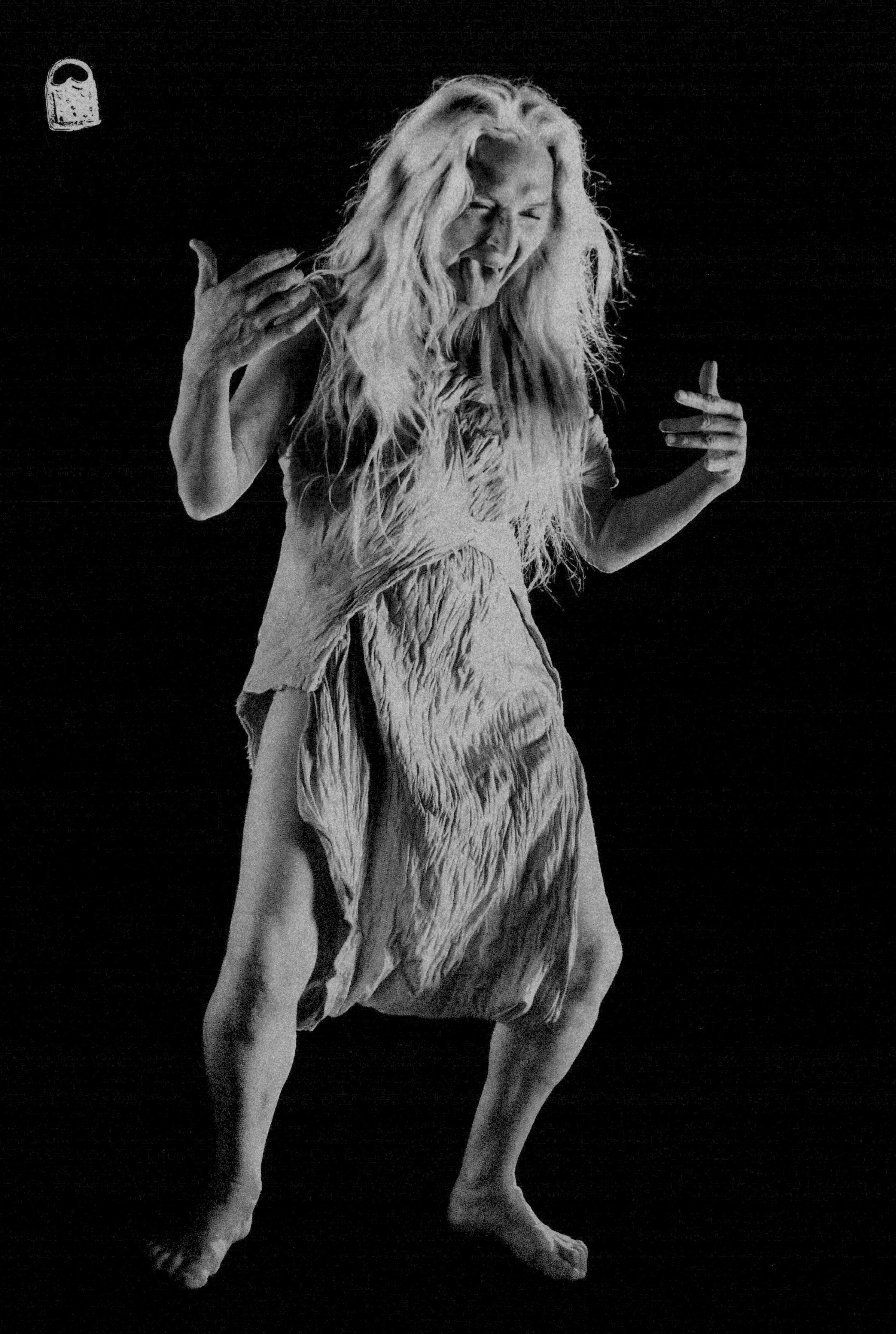

# O Children in God's Name
# Slay Not Your Mother!

Tina Kinsella

## What Was There, Before the Law?

Child, still thy nature bids thee love thy sire.
'Tis ever thus: some cleave unto their father,
Some more the mothers than the father love.
I pardon thee. In sooth, not all glad.

Euripides II: Electra, Orestes,
Iphigenia in Taurica, Andromache, Cyclops

Communicating mostly through the media of film by way of an appeal to the spectacular in the cinematic, Jesse Jones' artistic practice has often been interpreted as a political intervention in those social discourses that impinge upon and reproduce the subject in this tirelessly unending modernity. Always refusing the careless instrumentalisation of any specific political theory or ideology, Jones' work probes lost or discarded political possibilities which have been occluded by history, clouded by rhetoric and generally subject to sustained erasure under the logic of late capitalism. This gesturing towards the past to reimagine emancipatory potentialities for our contemporary moment is a refusal of nostalgia. Rather, Jones' archaeological manoeuvres through political potentialities lying dormant in the past invites the viewer-as-participator to inhabit the *present* as a space and place from which a politics for the future can be imagined and invented.

The body is always central to Jones' practice, being acknowledged as both a site of political imposition but also a field from which a politics might yet emerge. Evoking the pre-Oedipal soma that is *prior* to language, *before* the imposition of Law, *Tremble Tremble* (2017) poses the maternal body as a locus from which latent alternative political imaginaries may now be harvested and made manifest. This is a direct rejection of classical psychoanalytic interpretations of the dyadic mother-child relation whereby the maternal object, as signifier of the chaotic Real, must be abjected and abandoned so we can identify with the Law of the Father and thus become autonomous beings in the world.[1]

Via an appeal to the syntax of physical articulations we make in the world – sound, movement, tone, rhythm, voice – *Tremble Tremble* disturbs and re-enlivens the primary condition of corporeal assailability that all womb-born creatures share. Discrete divisions that we impose between ourselves and others are revealed as a human-made artifice, even a conceit, through the foregrounding of emergence from the body of our maternal origins: the very existence of which, necessarily, causes perturbations between self and other. Jones proposes our sojourn in the gargantuan maternal belly as an exemplary situation from which to reconsider political agency as resistance to the Patriarchal Law. The mythic figure of the giantess stands as visual and conceptual metaphor for the law of *In Utera Gigantae*, before which we, should, tremble. In Irish literature, the giant has longstanding associations with politics and the propulsions of market economy. Jonathan Swift's *Gulliver's Travels* (1726) offers a satirical take on the literary genre of traveller's tale whilst querying the tenets of philosophical humanism; the author asks the reader to consider whether it is goodness or corruption that lies at the heart of the human condition. Similarly, Oscar Wilde's *The Selfish Giant* (1888) seems to posit that owning private property is contrary and corruptive to human nature, and the only means by which man may regain his true nature is to relinquish his impulse towards accumulation and control.

Historical spectres still haunting the scene of contemporary Irish politics, Swift and Wilde's giants pose questions still pertinent to issues of Irish identity. But it is to the tradition of the giantess in Ireland's folkloric tradition that Jones turns for present day inspiration. We are recalled to the beautiful goddess-giantess of aristocratic bearing, Bébinn, who is closely associated with childbirth and the underworld, thereby being a maternal protector of the passage into life and the journey from it. And to Badb, also known as Badb Catha (battle crow); a giant war goddess who could transform herself into that dark bird in order to spread fear and confusion amongst soldiers on the battlefield and tilt the campaign

in favour of her preferred army. Through Jones' evocation
of the Irish mythological figure of the female giant-god-
dess we could turn to two of Leonora Carrington's works
*Down Below* (1941) and *The Giantess* (*The Guardian of
the Egg*) (c.1947). It was through her maternal line of
grandmother, mother and Irish nanny, that Carrington
learned about the rich lineage of the Mother Goddess
in Celtic myth and those tales of the dead who refuse
to remain in their place, who insistently breach the veil
between this life and the afterlife, between our world and the
otherworld (Tír na nÓg, Emain Ablach, Mag Mell). In *Down Below*
we find the tripartite Mother Goddess of maiden, mother, crone
who signals the passage from birth to death, and who, in this
painting, connects Carrington and her artistic creativity to the
otherworldly time space of childhood infused with structures
of maternal care. *The Giantess* is also thought to represent the
Mother Goddess. Though her form is colossal, she is neither terri-
fying, nor monstrous. Her visage conveys a sweet benevolence as
she holds a tiny egg, representing birth, in delicate hands. These
giantesses cluster in *Tremble Tremble*, weaving transgenerational
incantations to remind us we are *never* rid of other mothers. Time
past ushers into our time as an unshored-up maternal umbilical
cord connecting past, present, future.

## THE MATERNAL BODY
## AND THE VIOLENCE OF REPRESENTATION

Well may we weep! It was my sin, brother!
My fury was kindled as flame against
          her from whose womb I came.
Woe me, a daughter! And this my mother.[2]

As Andrea Liss remarks in her book *Feminist Art and the Maternal*
(2009), 'no body is more cruelly posed at the intersection of the
visible and the invisible, the public and the intimate, than the
maternal body'.[3] Her reflections concur with Rosemary Betterton's
observation that pregnancy as 'a process that occurs within a
woman's body … is structurally located in the personal and private

sphere'.⁴ But this personal sphere is also public property which is constructed and controlled through signifying practices, social and cultural discourses, and in this way the maternal body is 'subject to legal and medical constraint'.⁵ Betterton writes:

In western visual traditions, the maternal body has been conceptualised primarily as a container for the unborn child and its central modes of representation are the Christian maternal ideal, enshrined as the sacred vessel of divinity and the scientific concept of the pregnant body as a receptacle for new biological life.⁶

Motherhood and femininity are constructed through representational apparatuses and signifying practices riddled with assumptions of naturalness and passivity.⁷ Reconstructed as either a trope of idealised motherhood or considered as abstract container from which new life emerges, the maternal body is eviscerated of its own desire and divorced from its inherent eroticism.

Griselda Pollock foregrounds the erotic power of the 'monstrously sensual' maternal body in her discussion of Lucy Snowe's encounter with Artemisia Gentileschi's *Cleopatra* (1621-22) in Charlotte Brontë's novel *Villette* (1853).⁸ In the novel, Lucy Snowe remarks upon the 'scale of magnitude' in Gentileschi's *Cleopatra*, her 'affluence of flesh', the blaze of broad daylight around her as she reclines on a couch, and the utter lack of decorum she displays as, despite the abundance of her drapery, she nevertheless 'managed to make unsufficient raiment'.⁹ Miss Snowe is discovered in front of the painting by Monsieur Paul Emmanuel who redirects the young lady to four images entitled *La vie d'un femme* which she took as being 'cold and vapid as ghosts ... As bad in their way as the indolent gipsy-giantess.'¹⁰ The juxtaposition of these two images of femininity, one being desirous and rebellious, the other being virtuous and dutiful, produces a psychical dilemma for the female protagonist. Pollock notes that this vignette from Brontë's novel presents us with a feminist image for 'the fears and conflicts that assail those who have tried to conjoin creativity and femininity within patriarchal culture'.[11] As Pollock argues:

> All of us are already possessed by the culture within which we live, have been trained and educated, and practise as cultural analysts. We become 'personal' with implanted ideas and beliefs. We are trained to see canonically, and may ... speak with a borrowed voice, not even knowing what we do, and from whom the voice is borrowed.[12]

Lucy Snowe's response to both Gentileschi's *Cleopatra* and the images of women's duty conveyed in *La vie d'un femme* reflect a particularly feminine ambivalence when women are presented with images of themselves. Perplexed by Monsieur Emmanuel's intervention in front of Gentileschi's painting, Lucy Snowe asks him what he thinks of this depiction of Cleopatra. Her male companion replies that the painting shows a beautiful woman with the figure of an empress, the form of Juno, but not a person he would want as a wife, nor as a daughter or as a sister. The clear intent of Monsieur Emmanuel's comment is to inform the young woman that she must value chastity, purity, duty, and refrain from any celebration of such effusive and abundant femininity should she wish to secure a husband in the future. The visual representation of a mature, maternal body is refused as a site of potential identification for Lucy Snowe and is, instead, transformed into an eroticised site for the purposes of Monsieur Emmanuel's male gaze. This scene from Brontë's novel aptly demonstrates how women are commanded to look at themselves as though from the man's position. But it also asks us to consider the social dynamics within which feminine desire is produced by a culture that singularly privileges masculine desire and identity.

This privileging of the masculine position is evident in Sigmund Freud's analytic of uncanny anxiety (1919).[13] Whilst Freud acknowledges the maternal womb as a place of homely origin, he proposes that this once familiar place-space must be subject to primary repression. Retrospectively, the maternal body becomes the ground from which psychical material, stored in the unconscious, is forged. When maternal material returns, it does so *aprés coup,* manifesting in displaced aesthetic affects masquerading in ghoulish phantasmagoria such as *doppelgängers* and mechanical almost-human doubles that threaten the subject's sense of a sovereign and singular self. Powering the engine of such uncanny phantasmagoria are *mutterleibsphantasein,* the 'fantasy of living in the womb' which, Freud argues, rely on a 'certain lasciviousness'.[14] This desire towards the mother's body, Freud firmly suggests, should be sublimated and redirected into artistic endeavours. The maternal body, thus displaced, becomes the container for all that provokes horror, anxiety, the threatened collapse of one's sovereign boundaries, and must thereby be negated, fetishised, or put to psychical death through the very processes of sublimation that create art, but all of this exclusively within an economy of male creativity, desire and inspiration.

In her work on infant anxiety, Melanie Klein discusses Maurice Ravel's opera *L'enfant et les sortilèges: Fantaisie lyrique en deux parties* (1925) which tells the story of a naughty child who, having been scolded by his mother, sets about destroying the objects in his room.[15] In turn, the objects become animated and reprimand the boy for his cruelty. In response to Ravel's opera, Klein writes that the child's whole world is 'transformed into the mother's body' which 'is in hostile array against the child and persecutes him'.[16] Emily Apter suggests that in Klein's text the:

> Super-scaled and super phallic ... giant maternal corpus is broken down into anatomical and sartorial part-objects, each convertible to domestic objects – armchair, cushion, table, chair – that receive the brunt of the child's anger after he is denied his wish to go to the park.[17]

Klein's analysis of Ravel's opera supports the relationship that Freud details between the return of the repressed maternal body in uncannily animated containers, thus highlighting the anxiety the giant maternal body produces in a phallic economy that privileges the shoring up of corporeal and psychical boundaries. From this perspective, separation from the maternal body is necessary to become an autonomous subject, with agency. With this move the maternal body is consigned forever as object. In this sense, the maternal corpus designates that limit or tipping point which henceforth defines the relationship between self and other, subject and object, self and world.

## BETWEEN THE SELF AND THE OTHER

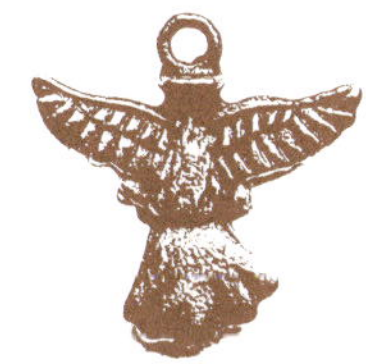

Lately sparkling hosts,
Come fill my dreams, descending,
On fiery beams,
I've seen 'em come clear down,
Where our poor bodies lay,
Soothe us gently and say,
'Gonna wipe all your tears away'.
And still I hear their whisper ...[18]

In her book *Horrorism: Naming Contemporary Violence* (2011), Adriana Cavarero quotes Louis-Ferdinand Céline's novel *Voyage au bout de la nuit* (1932):[19]

> This body of ours, a travesty of agitated and banal molecules, revolts all the time against this atrocious farce of continued existence. They want to disperse out into the universe, our molecules, as rapidly as possible, these dear ones! They suffer from being only 'us', cuckolds of infinity.[20]

Of course, this novel was written in the aftermath of the first World War during which millions of young men's bodies were violently obliterated: quite literally dispersed into little molecules distributed throughout the universe. But, for Cavarero, this passage of Céline's asks us to consider the structural relation between individuality and collectivity. Céline's advocacy for an ecstatic disappearance of the *I* into a violent and organic *we* can be considered as antidote to the contemporary anxiety surrounding the 'loss of one's own I'.[21] We can also understand this polarity between the singular *I* and multiplicitous *we* as a potent metaphor for the relationship between self and other, so is there not a problem with posing these two categories in opposition to each other? Cavarero points towards Jacques Derrida's definition of the 'metaphysics of presence' which relays how our conceptual thinking is framed through binary concepts. According to Derrida, the metaphysics of presence creates an epistemological hierarchy that privileges presence over absence, subject over object, mind over matter, culture over nature. The resulting epistemological cul-de-sac, Derrida argues, is that the masculine is situated on the side of presence, subject, mind and culture whereas the feminine is displaced to the position of absence, object, matter, nature.

*Tremble Tremble* demands that we revisit this privileging of the male mind over the female body so to recuperate the maternal body as a field of horizon from which to radically reinvent the now and the future. Jones' proposition chimes with the thought of artist and psychoanalytic theorist, Bracha L. Ettinger, who elaborates pregnancy and birthing as models for co-emergence through which we can consider *'futurity in the now'* as a non-phallic perspective from which to radically rethink the ethical relation between self, Other and world.[22] Ettinger proposes the pregnant woman as a subjectivising agency for the not-yet-infant as 'presubject, partial-subject' who is co-emerging into life in a relation of 'transgressive shareability' alongside the mother, otherwise known as becoming-mother (becoming-m/Other).[23] This relation of emergence donates an excess of primary compassion which indexes 'openness to the world' that is formed by way of late intrauterine affective exchanges and attunements between the not-yet-born infant (otherwise known as I) and the infant's non-I who is the 'm/Other as almost-Other which is non-conscious, preconceptual and pre-identitarian'.[24] In response to Freud's analytic of uncanny anxiety (*Unheimliche Angst*), Ettinger argues that the becoming-m/Other (as almost-Other to begin with) is 'not the site of rejected psychic materials', but is a space-place filled with the potential of 'continuity and a shared affective trembling' that bequeaths the facility for primordial affective arousals exchanged during late pregnancy that are not only anxiety, and which can be understood as primary compassion and primary awe.[25] As Freud detailed uncanny anxiety as an aesthetic affect, so does Ettinger relate uncanny compassion and uncanny awe to aesthetics by way of unfolding how these primary affects can be aroused during our experience of beauty and the sublime in our encounter with some artworks:

> Beauty moves toward the Sublime and a Sublime moves toward Beauty, intermixed with knowledge without rejection or fusion at either aesthetic pole, when our cognition and our defences are suspended for a while, in respect.[26]

As both men and women issue from the maternal womb in their very first instance, these primary affects remain as a potentiality for both sexes, regardless of gender and sexuality. Ettinger's insights offer a way through the impasse in thought defined by Cavarero in her discussion of the seemingly irresolvable tussle between the sovereign *I* and the assailable *we*. For what Ettinger invites us to consider is that there is an almost-alterity installed in the self by way of the most profound emergence of the subject from the maternal womb in the body of a pregnant woman. As such, Ettinger's model of co-emergence in the maternal body offers a radical model by which to think about the relation between self and other whereby the *I* does not collapse into a boundless *we*. In turn, this model of affective co-emergence offers a pragmatic architecture for Jones' call to think of the maternal womb as a copious space from which to imagine alternative political possibilities. Ettinger's proposal of uncanny compassion and awe as primary aesthetic affects that touch upon the beautiful and the sublime, allow us to consider a primordial ethical disposition within the human towards that which is other than the sovereign self. As Jones' work gestures towards lost or forgotten possibilities lying dormant in the past, so the maternal body that had been consigned to representative, signifying and theoretical oblivion, can be habilitated as a conceptual apparatus from which to reimagine the future based upon the principles of awe and compassion.

Philip Pullman's trilogy of fantasy novels, *His Dark Materials* (1995-2000) details a cosmo-verse in which all children have a *daemon* companion with the protean facility to shapeshift into any number of animal creatures. However, once the child transits through adolescence and into adulthood, the *daemon* stabilises to assume the shape and characteristics of one animal only. Lyra, the main female character, asks 'Why do daemons have to settle?' Referring to her *daemon*, she muses 'I want Pantalaimon to be able to change for ever. So does he.' But an adult warns her: 'when your *daemon* settles, you'll know what kind of person you are'. Lyra and her *daemon* are under threat of the adjunct of the patriarchal Law that demands fixity between oneself and the Other so that identity may be established. Yet Lyra's words testify to the affective connection established at birth between the child and its *daemon*. Lyra and Pantalaimon are attuned to each other's feelings precisely because of this invisible umbilicus through which part of the child is in the *daemon* and part of the *daemon* is in the child. I am reminded of the manner in which Judee Sill introduced her song 'The Kiss' on an episode of BBC2's *The Old Grey Whistle Test* in 1973 when she claimed that the lyrics of this song were about 'the union of opposites that we all have and the kiss is a symbol of the union'.[27] As Sill's lyrics evoke the *anima* and *animus* as analogue for an otherness always, already installed in the self, so Pullman's child-*daemon* dyad provokes our thought to contemplate our inherent capacity to respond to what is not quite the self. Both perspectives resonate with Ettinger's claims for that part within us which ever was an almost-alterity, what she terms an Othereity, that donates the capacity for response to others from the position of a foundational ethicality.

## THE MATERNAL BODY AS A SITE FOR THE REINVENTION OF POLITICAL IMAGINARIES?

… death lurks in the throats of women.[28]

The giantess of Jesse Jones' *Tremble Tremble* evokes the largesse of the maternal body, which in turn provokes the meaning donation of the maternal womb that Ettinger outlines. But with Jones' work for the Venice Biennale we are also reminded of the ancient Sheelagh-na-Gigs, those stone carvings which depict a female figure opening and exposing her enormous vulva.

Like the Tripartite Mother Goddess previously mentioned, the Sheelaghs are thought to be symbols of birth, fertility and death that were positioned over threshold spaces such as doorways and window openings, thus providing a symbolic reference for those liminal phases of birthing and dying. In her book on the Sheelagh-na-Gigs, Barbara Freitag discusses the work of William Borlase, a scholar writing about Irish dolmens at the end of the nineteenth century who suggested that these figures should be named 'sheelanagyg' or 'Sheela na Gyg'.[29] Borlase argued that 'gyg' is the name in Norse for a female *lötun* or giantess and he thereby interprets Sheela-na-Gyg to mean 'Image of the Giantess'.[30] In support of his claims, Borlase references an Irish legend about a giantess called Sheela who, following a row with her equally giant husband, seized their marital bed and flung it at him. Mid-flight the devil intervened and turned the bed into stone, so that when it landed on Sheela's husband it crushed him to death and to this day he rests beneath the hag's bed.[31]

This parable not only reminds us of the giantess as an allegorical landscape within which Jones' present work sits, it calls our attention to the consequences for the human when the maternal voice is silenced. As Cavarero observes 'the voice stands in opposition to language' – that is, to the disciplining codes of language, to grammar and syntax, to the 'Law of the Father' that separates the infant from the mother by consigning the child to the logic of individuality.[32] We can now return to the second part of Ravel's opera, during which the young boy's bedroom is transformed into a garden filled with animals and plants which have been tortured or abused by the child. The animals and plants set upon the boy but when a squirrel gets hurt in the affray, the fighting stops. The little boy bandages the squirrel's wounds and the other animals help him. It is only when the child's compassion is aroused that he can sing Maman, thereby literally ventriloquising the archaic maternal voice. The opera ends with the reunion of the child with his mother.

As Nicole Loraux observes, the point of greatest vulnerability for women in ancient Greek tragedy was the *derē*, the soft region of the throat from which the voice issues. The throat is the bodily region where death comes to young girls chosen for sacrifice such as the Trojan princess, Polyxena, or Agamemnon and Clytemnestra's daughter, Iphigenia, whose throat was slit against her mother's will so that the Greek fleet might sail to Troy. It is from the throat that Clytemnestra's voice issues to beseech her two surviving children, Electra and Orestes, to stave her death: 'O children in God's name slay not your mother!'[33] And it is into his mother's throat that Orestes thrusts the blade that kills her. Just as the heroic Odysseus must 'stop up his ears' against the song of the Sirens lest they lure him to a watery tomb, so must the son's ear make mute that first maternal voice that signals an unthinkable return to the maternal body in a phallic economy and patriarchal culture that can only consider womb as tomb.

But the voice of Jones' giantess that recalls us to the orality of the early maternal scene, also returns us to that watery womb time-space-place before semantics, before signification process, before the phallus. Buoyed by the rhythm of the maternal voice that chants the law of *In Utera Gigantae*, we are recalled to rehabilitate our ethical sensibilities and dream up alternative political imaginaries by way of a maternal invitation. Posed as a political gesture, the law of *In Utera Gigantae* issues an edict to consider the oubliette time-space of the maternal womb as a site of possibility that may yet yield bonds of obligation to the living.

1.
Kristeva, J. (1991) *Women Analyze Women in France, England, and the United States*, Baruch, E. and Serrano, L. J. (eds), New York and London, Columbia University Press, pp. 136-7.

2.
*Euripides II: Electra, Orestes, Iphigenia in Taurica, Andromache, Cyclops*, (1978) (trans. A. S. Way), Cambridge, Massachusetts, Loeb Classical Library, p. 10. The words cited are spoken by Electra to her brother Orestes directly after he murders their mother Clytemnestra.

3.
Liss, A. (2009) *Feminist Art and the Maternal*, Minneapolis and London, University of Minnesota Press, p. xxiii.

4.
Betterton, R. (2009) 'Maternal Bodies in Visual Culture', *Studies in the Maternal*, vol. 1, no. 1.

5.
Ibid.

6.
Ibid.

7.
Liss, A. (2009) *Feminist Art and the Maternal*, Minneapolis and London, University of Minnesota Press, p. xi.

8.
Pollock, G. (1999) *Differencing the Canon: Feminist Desire and the Writing of Art's Histories*, London and New York, Routledge, p. 156.

9.
Charlotte Brontë's *Villette* was first published in 1853 under the pseudonym Currer Bell.

10.
Brontë, C. *Villette*.

11.
Pollock, G. *Differencing the Canon*, p. 156.

12.
Pollock, G. *Differencing the Canon*.

13.
Freud, S. (2003 [1919]) 'The Uncanny', *The Uncanny* (trans. D. McLintock), London and New York, Penguin, pp. 121-162.

14.
Freud, S. 'The Uncanny'.

15.
Melanie Klein's discussion of Ravel's opera unfolds in her text from 1929, 'Infantile Anxiety Situations Reflected in a Work of Art and the Creative Impulse'.

16.
Ibid.

17.
Apter, E. (2006) 'Maternal Fetishism', *Perversion: Psychoanalytic Perspectives - Perspectives on Psychoanalysis*, Nobus, D. and Downing, L. (eds), London and New York, Karnac, p. 256.

18.
Lyrics from 'The Kiss' (1973) by Judee Sill.

19.
Cavarero, A. (2011) *Horrorism: Naming Contemporary Violence* (trans. W. McCuaig), New York, Columbia University Press.

20.
Céline, L-F. (1932) *Voyage au bout de la nuit* (Voyage to the End of the Night), Paris, Librairie Gallimard, p. 337. It should be noted that Céline had fascist and anti-semitic tendencies, and the quotation from his novel is by no means an endorsement of his politics.

21.
Cavarero, A. *Horrorism*, pp. 49-50.

22.
Ettinger, B. L. (2006) 'From Proto-Ethical Compassion to Responsibility: Besideness and the Three Primal Mother-Phantasies of Not-Enoughness, Devouring and Abandonment', *Athena: Philosophical Studies*, no. 2, p. 102.

23.
Ibid, p. 104.

24.
Ibid, p. 122.

25.
Ettinger, B. L. (2011) 'Uncanny Awe, Uncanny Compassion and Matrixial Transjectivity Beyond Uncanny Anxiety', *French Literature Series*, vol. xxxviii, p. 4.

26.
Ibid, p. 12.

27.
See: youtube.com/watch?v=0feFedDW_iQ

28.
Loraux, N. (1987) *Tragic Ways of Killing a Woman* (trans. A. Forster), Cambridge and London, Harvard University Press, p. 52.

29.
Freitag, B. (2004) *Sheela-na-Gigs: Unravelling an Enigma*, Oxford and New York, Routledge, p. 55.

30.
Ibid.

31.
Freitag, B. *Sheela-na-Gigs*.

32.
Cavarero, A. (1995) *For More than One Voice: Toward a Philosophy of Vocal Expression* (trans. P. A. Kottman), Stanford, Stanford University Press, p. 132.

33.
*Euripides II*, p. 10. The words cited are spoken by Clytemnestra to her daughter Electra before the mother is murdered by her son, Orestes.

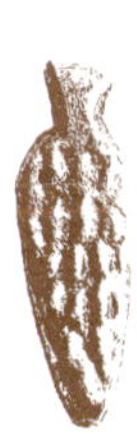

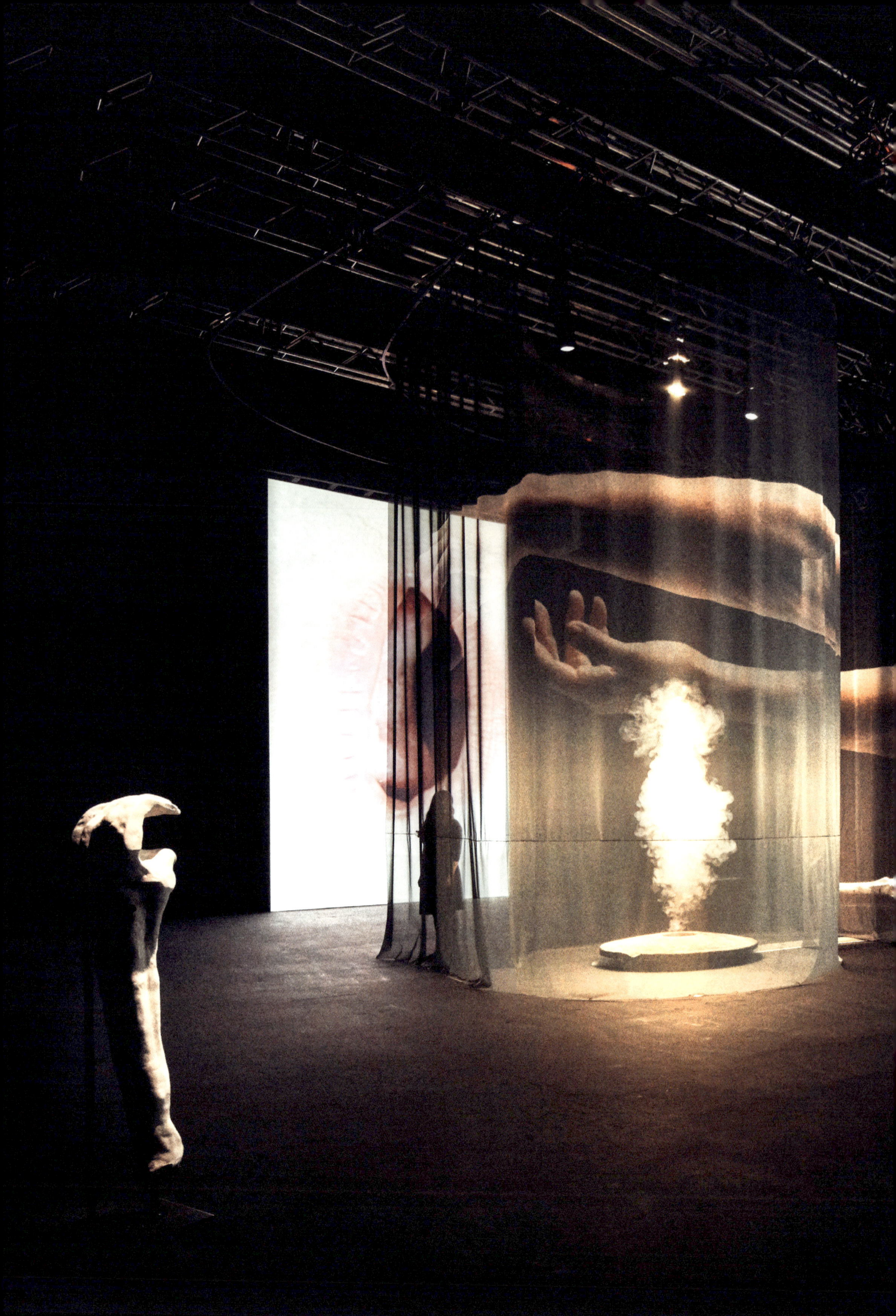

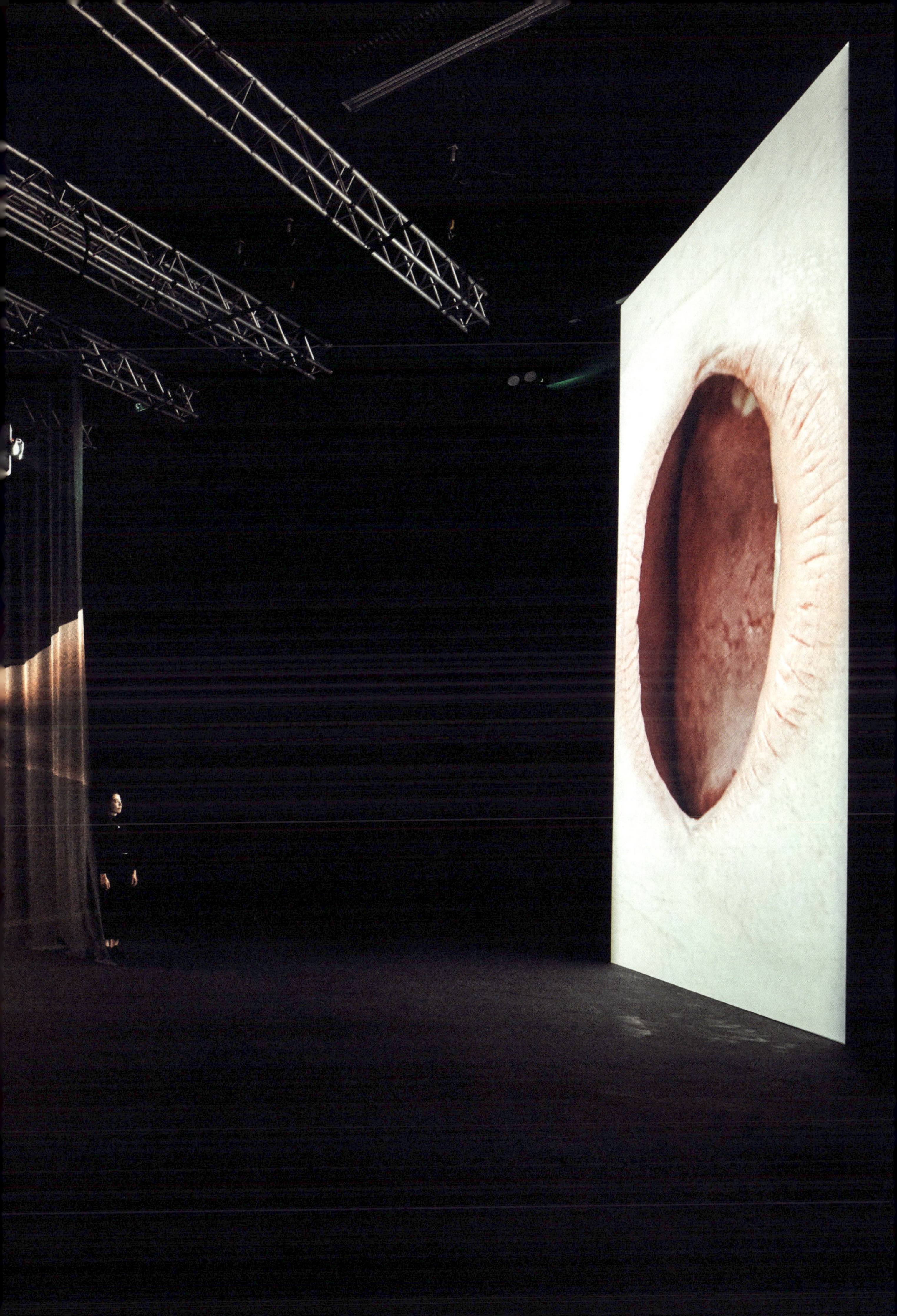

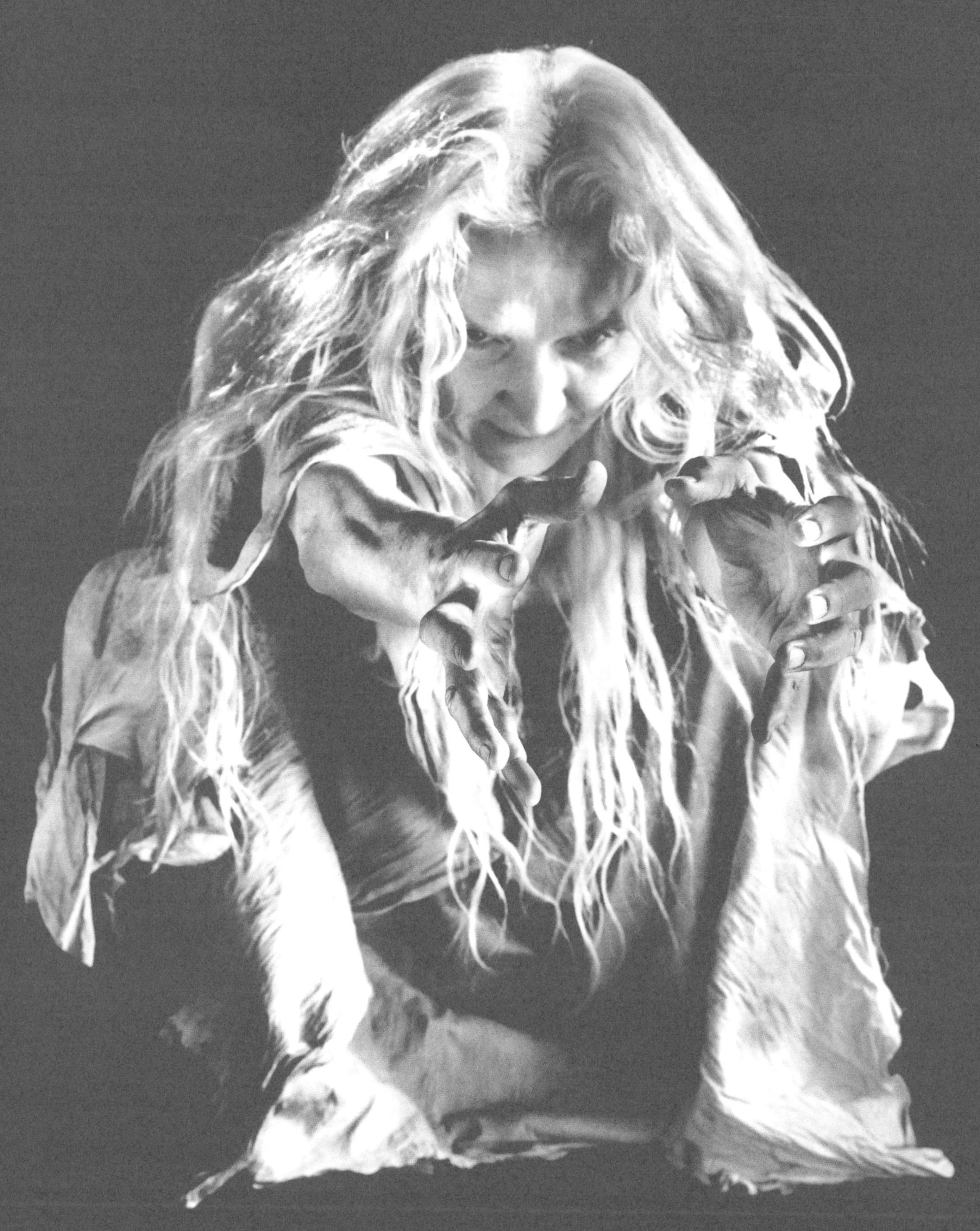

# A Finger, a Hand-breadth, a Span, a Foot

Lisa Godson

'Matter of factness' is finally dispatched, and in the face of the huge images across the walls of houses, where toothpaste and cosmetics lie handy for giants, sentimentality is restored to health and liberated in American style, just as people whom nothing moves or touches any longer are taught to cry again by films.[1]

1 For *No More Fun and Games* (Dublin City Gallery, the Hugh Lane, 2016), Jesse Jones established a 'Feminist Parasite Institution' that dwelt within and fed from its host. I was one among a curatorial collective, and we examined a list of all the artworks by women within the gallery's collection, and then forced the mining of some from the storerooms into the light, creating an exhibition of this hidden work within Jones' show. Among them was a revelatory oil painting by Isobel Gloag (1865-1917), last displayed in the 1930s. *The Woman with the Puppets* (1915) lies back, raising a flaccid little man by her left hand, trailing another (carelessly) on the floor by her right. A tiny lawyer lolls against her bed, and two other miniatures flop on the woman's bedside table. By the measure of her body, they are slightly under a cubit tall. Unlike puppets that might be filled with the 'frail, excitable life of the hand',[2] the woman takes no care to animate them. She is naked, the lawyer puppet is in a wig and gown, others in formal evening wear. For visitors to the exhibition in 2016, the painting seemed to invert gender power relations – these men in various forms of powerful, codified dress, treated as insignificant toys by a giantess. Although the painting was listed on the official inventory of the gallery, it was a 'forgotten' work, one of the 'rejected bits and pieces', that Mary Douglas describes in relation to things that are incompletely categorised as waste, 'out of place' in the creation of another kind of order.[3]

2    Visitors to *No More Fun and Games* were directed from the Parasite Institution's reception desk by a massive image of an arm that terminated in a gesturing hand, one finger pointing. It was printed on a 12-metre-wide curtain that travelled along a track and snaked throughout the galleries, coming to rest in the room where the painting by Gloag was installed alongside other works from the gallery's collection. What often happens in the depiction of the gigantic, Susan Stewart tells us, is a 'severing of the synecdoche from its referent, or whole'.[4] In other words, one portion of the gigantic cannot stand fully for its entirety, parts of the body become things in themselves. And so, in Gulliver's travels to Brobdingnag, the breast of the Queen that 'stood prominent six feet, and could not be less than sixteen in circumference' seems 'separable' from the body, Gulliver recounting how 'no object ever disgusted me so much as the sight of her monstrous breast, which I cannot tell what to compare with'.[5] When faced with giants, the 'partial vision of the observer prohibits closure of the object'.[6] Unable to apprehend the entirety, we are only conscious of parts, of unfathomable reach.

3    If, as Stewart suggests, the gigantic might be considered as a metaphor for the 'abstract authority of the state',[7] this seems apposite in relation to Jones' *In the Shadow of the State* (2016), a multi-event collaboration with Sarah Browne. This was commissioned as one of the national art projects to mark the centenary of the 1916 Easter Rising, the armed rebellion against British rule that ultimately led to Irish national independence. The notion of living in its 'shadow' suggests not only the gigantism of the State in terms of scale, but its ungraspable nature. Through their project, Jones and Browne explored the actions of the State from the perspective of the female body.

They developed 'tactics and strategies to move from one historical moment to another,'[8] attempting to materialise the State's effects on the body through substances (*Of Milk and Marble*), through instruments (*The Truncheon and the Speculum*) and through legal arrangements (*The Touching Contract*). The projects were deeply collaborative, the artists working with experts in law, material culture, sound, medicine and those who had been directly affected by the violence of the touch of the State. The permeable, co-evolved nature of the project asserted an alternative to the abstract, gigantic shadow cast by the State, suggesting instead the values of the Irish axiom 'ar scáth a chéile a mhaireann na daoine' (in the shade of each other, the people live).

4 In the version of the 1916 Rising that was officially memorialised in 2016, the role of female revolutionaries was afforded more prominence than ever before. This *re-remembering* or *unforgetting* was partly a matter of redress, as the 'official' memory of the Rising had previously downplayed the role of women. As Mona Ozouf writes in relation to national commemoration 'the myth of origin is also the instrument of a teleology'.[9] The Irish State that came into political being in 1922 so greatly diminished women that the Rising could only work as a foundational moment if the memory of female insurgents was off-stage. From 1922, successive legislative acts and a broader nationalist and religious discourse severely curtailed the ability of women to be involved in public life in Ireland, and reached deep into their private lives. Their presence was shrunken, belittled, contracted. The geographers Una Crowley and Rob Kitchin have identified 21 specific reports and government acts that were passed between 1922 and 1937 and that produced a 'dense spatialised grid of discipline, reform and self-regulation'[10] for Irish women, including laws that deprived them of the right to sit on juries, to be employed in certain industries, to use contraception and that allowed them to be incarcerated if they had children outside marriage. The 'fate of women within society was sealed' by the Irish Constitution (1937) which enacted that 'mothers shall not be obliged by economic necessity to engage in labour to the neglect of their duties in the home' (article 41.2.2), confining them to the reproductive and domestic.[11] This emphasis is upheld by the Eighth Amendment to the Irish Constitution (1983) that equates and reduces the life of the mother with that of her unborn child, forcing thousands of women every year to either travel outside the country for abortions or undergo unwanted pregnancies. The felt, bodily reality of such diminution of women was made manifest throughout *In the Shadow of the State*, and is countered in *Tremble Tremble*. In both, the re-ordering of the political imaginary is central, but whereas *In the Shadow of the State* excavated and performed specific moments from the past, *Tremble Tremble* posits an alternative future.

5   Towards the end of Lewis Carroll's *Alice's Adventures in Wonderland* (1865), Alice is pleased to find herself in a court of law. In a world of incoherence and unreason, she expects that here, at least, sanity and logic will prevail. But the trial is marked by disorder, procedures are improvised, concepts of innocence and guilt are toyed with. And besides, Alice herself is starting to grow. She is so eager to give evidence, to participate in the institutional process, she forgets her scale and knocks over the jury box. And thus the King prohibits her from speaking:

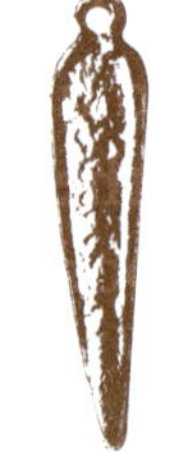

'Rule Forty-two.
*All persons more than
a mile high to leave the court.'*

Everybody looked at Alice.

'*I'm* not a mile high,' said Alice.

'You are,' said the King.
'Nearly two miles high,'
added the Queen.

'Well, I shan't go, at any rate,'
said Alice: 'besides, that's not a
regular rule: you invented it just now.'

'It's the oldest rule in the book,'
said the King.

'Then it ought to be Number One,'
said Alice.[12]

If
her shrinking
and expanding throughout
her adventures is a metaphor for maturity,
for moving from dependence to autonomy, this is the
moment that Alice realises that the legal system will not provide

truth and order, and her own agency must be asserted for her survival. Rule forty-two, as Alice notes, is prejudiced and arbitrary, not foundational or natural.

6   Stewart describes the giant as 'a violator of boundary and rule; an overabundance of the natural and hence an affront to cultural systems'.[13] Through materialising a female giant in *Tremble Tremble*, Jesse Jones expresses the need for disruption of the received order. She traces and forecasts a genealogy for those who have been systematically excluded from the rewards of modernity, those who have fought and continue to struggle to overturn injustice, whether that be the denial of wages for housework in 1970s Italy, or bodily autonomy in contemporary Ireland. In his recent work, the philosopher Michel Serres celebrates the information revolution and its potential for establishing a new politics of networked young females who can reject old forms of authority, for whom all the old *belongings* are dying: 'Army, nation, church … These are abstractions, flying above our heads like cardboard fetishes.'[14] For this he calls on the totemic figure of Thumbelina, partly because of how the young swipe and activate their screens, but also because, for now, they have been overlooked. The colossal arms in *Tremble Tremble* are a materialisation of strength at another scale – not only through their specific, measurable size but because of what they might be attached to, what they might make, what they point to, what they beckon us for.


1.
Benjamin, W. (2016 [1926]) 'The Unclouded Eye', *One Way Street* (trans. E. Jephcott), Cambridge, Massachusetts, Harvard University Press, p. 77.

2.
Connor, S. (2009) *The Book of Skin*, London, Reaktion, p. 140.

3.
Douglas, M. (1966) *Purity and Danger: An Analysis of Concepts of Pollution and Taboo*, London, Routledge, p. 160.

4.
Stewart, S. (1984) *On Longing: Narratives of the Miniature, the Gigantic, the Souvenir, the Collection*, Durham, Duke University Press, p. 89.

5.
Swift, J. (1992 [1726]) *Gulliver's Travels*, London, Wordsworth Editions, p. 68.

6.
Stewart, S. *On Longing*, p. 89.

7.
Ibid, p. xii.

8.
*The Theatre of Change Symposium day one – Panel: The Body of the State* (2016), Jesse Jones and Sarah Browne presentation. Available at youtube.com/watch?v=2K7vhnnq620

9.
Ozouf, M. (1988) *Festivals and the French Revolution*, Cambridge, Massachusetts, Harvard University Press, p. 276.

10.
Crowley, U. and Kitchin, R. (2008) 'Producing "Decent Girls": Governmentality and the Moral Geographies of Sexual Conduct in Ireland (1922–1937)', *Gender, Place and Culture*, vol. 15, no. 4, pp. 355-72, p. 355.

11.
Ibid, p. 355.

12.
Carroll, L. (2001 [1865]) *Alice in Wonderland*, New York, Scholastic, p. 149.

13.
Stewart, S. *On Longing*, p. 73.

14.
Serres, M. (2014) *Thumbelina: The Culture and Technology of Millennials*, London, Rowman & Littlefield International, p. 56.

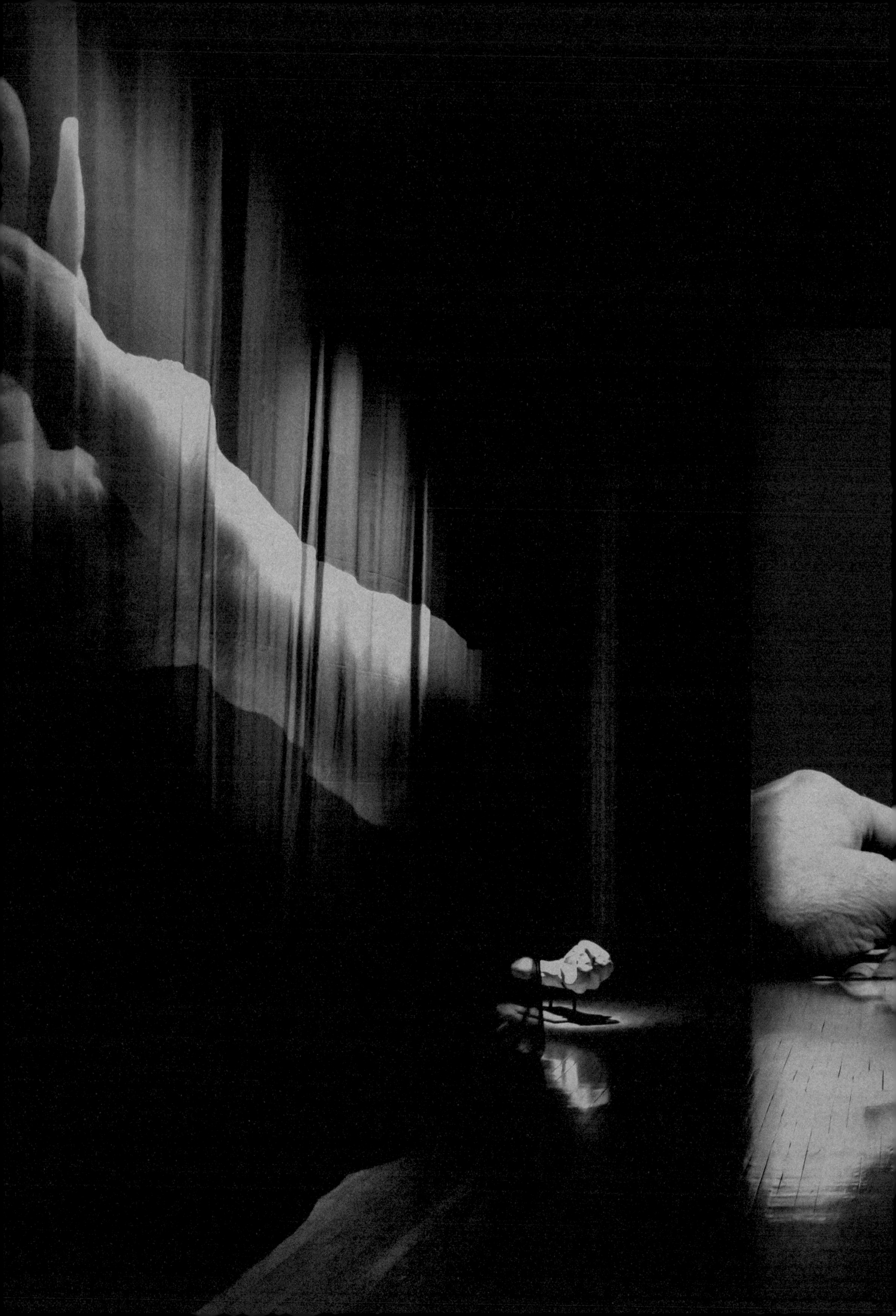

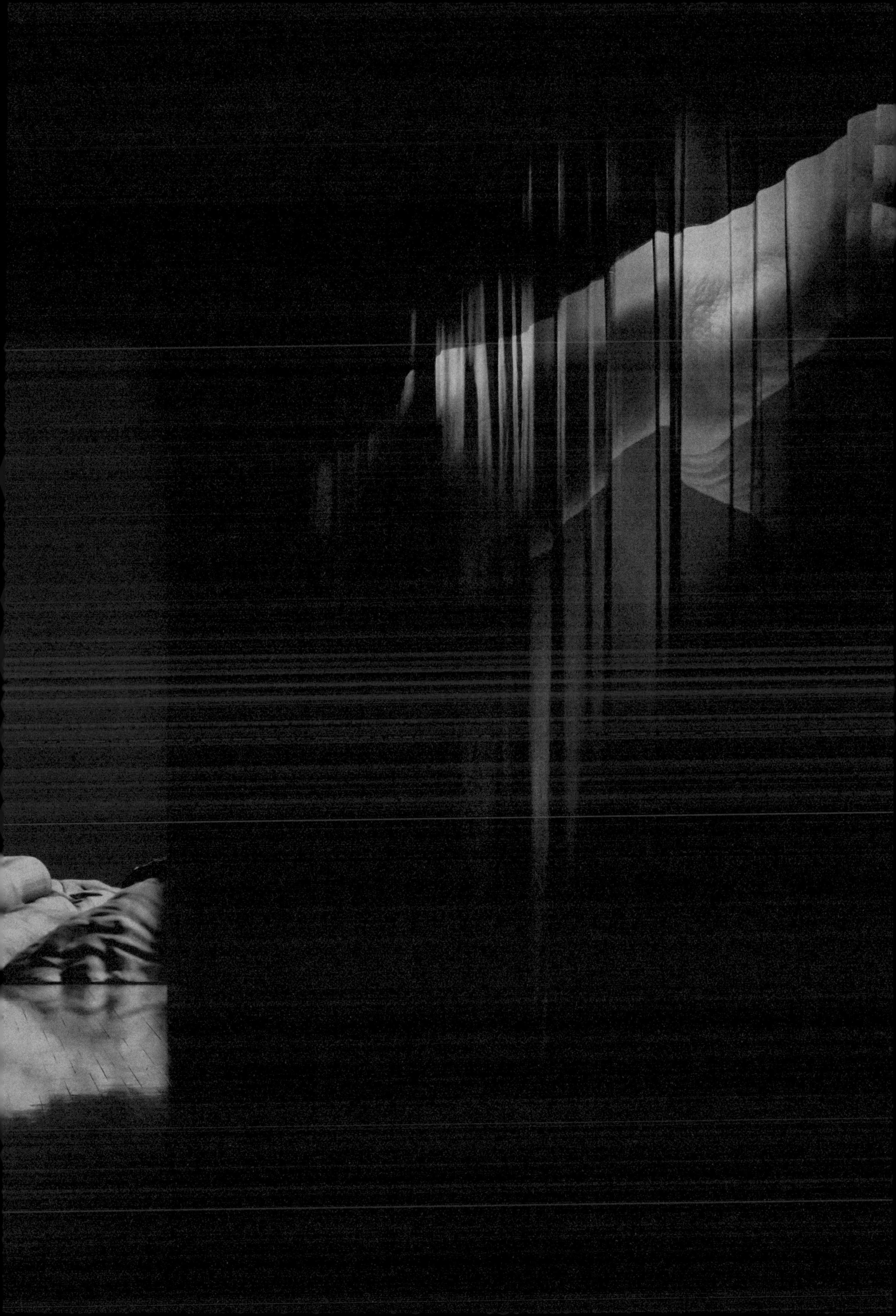

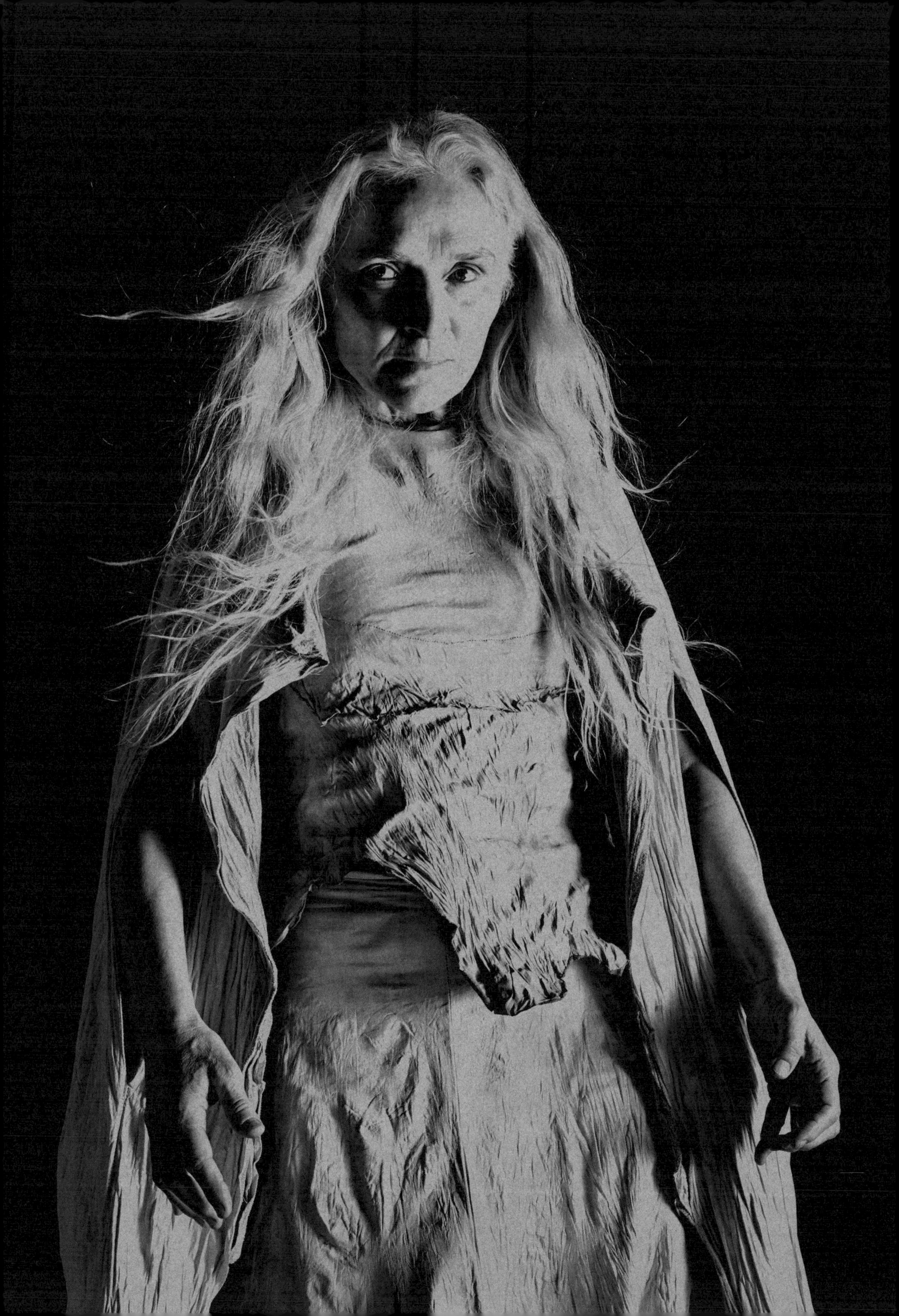

# Did We Disturb You Good People?

Tessa Giblin

This is a story about an artwork that was made in an environment of change. It was carried by seismic shifts in Irish cultural and political history and it is about how artists, activists, politicians and the media grasped the nature of artworks and their potential to motivate, empower and effect change.

> How can I represent my country when my
> country doesn't represent me?
> Jesse Jones, May 2017

When the Irish Pavilion was opened at the Venice Biennale in 2017 (the only biennale or art event that includes national representation), these were the piercing words with which Jesse Jones concluded her opening remarks. She was describing what it meant to be asked to represent her country – and the internal conflict that arose in relation to present-day Ireland. Jones, like many Irish women and men, was agitating for change. She was agitating for the right to determine the future of her own body; agitating to repeal the Eighth Amendment to the Constitution of Ireland. But at the time she opened the pavilion, her country still withheld these rights and women's bodies were bound by a law that equated their life to that of their unborn foetuses.

But the artwork wasn't made in May 2017. It began life almost two years earlier, when Ireland was celebrating the first time any country had legalised same-sex marriage by referendum in 2015. This had happened within a complex national debate that ultimately reframed Ireland's cultural relationship with its deep Catholic roots and paved the way for equal rights around marriage and a more tolerant, fair and accepting outlook on LGBTQ+ issues.

At a National Campaign for the Arts meeting at Project Arts Centre (around this time) we were addressed by Brian Sheehan, one of the lead campaigners for marriage equality, who shared the

62

journey that he and many others had been on in trying to find the language, or ideas that would motivate the kind of change they wanted. They needed to find a way to make gay marriage an idea that mattered to everyone, as not everyone was ready to fight for gay rights. But they understood that the campaign needed to be based on core values – and equality is something that matters to Irish people. In other contexts where same-sex marriage had been legalised through an act of parliament, it requires half the police force to protect the annual Pride march. I distinctly remember him saying: 'We knew that this was not the outcome we wanted. If we were going to win, we needed to bring the hearts and minds of people along with us.'

I will never forget that address, as within it you can also hear the whispers and murmurings of how artists were going to help to repeal the Eighth Amendment – by bringing the hearts and minds of people along with them. What was also motivating for us was the incredible, compelling influence of Italian scholar, teacher and activist, Silvia Federici.

Silvia Federici's writing has located the historic oppression of women in a history of capitalism, and uniquely studied the reason that women needed to be oppressed within this system. *Caliban and the Witch* (2004) represents this story very well, often returning to the body (all bodies) as the site of exploitation. In

> writing about the witch trials and the oppression of women, Federici addresses this historical moment: 'The body has been for women in capitalist society what the factory has been for male waged workers: the primary ground of their exploitation and resistance, as the female body has been appropriated by the State and men and forced to function as a means for the reproduction and accumulation of labour.'[1] If you wanted to control capital in the twelfth century, then you needed to control the source of the labour force: women, and their reproductivity. During this period, midwifery was taken from women and into the control of the Church or

State and saw religious proclamations against acts of male homosexuality as 'non-reproductive sex'. Here we find the roots of the oppression of women that would find its height in the hysteria of the witch trials, and as *Tremble Tremble* shows, that haunts us still, with modern Ireland being no exception.

As Jesse Jones set about writing scripts and preparing sculptures – and together we developed the scenography that drew together the visual arts, film and theatre, the movement in Ireland to overturn the ban on abortion grew more intense. All around the country, campaigns were building to repeal the Eighth Amendment. Politicians such as Michael D. Higgins had loudly contested its inception in 1983 and many tireless warriors had been working to repeal it since it was adopted as law in 1983. By 2017, some 34 years later, momentum had grown and Ireland was riding a cultural wave of change.

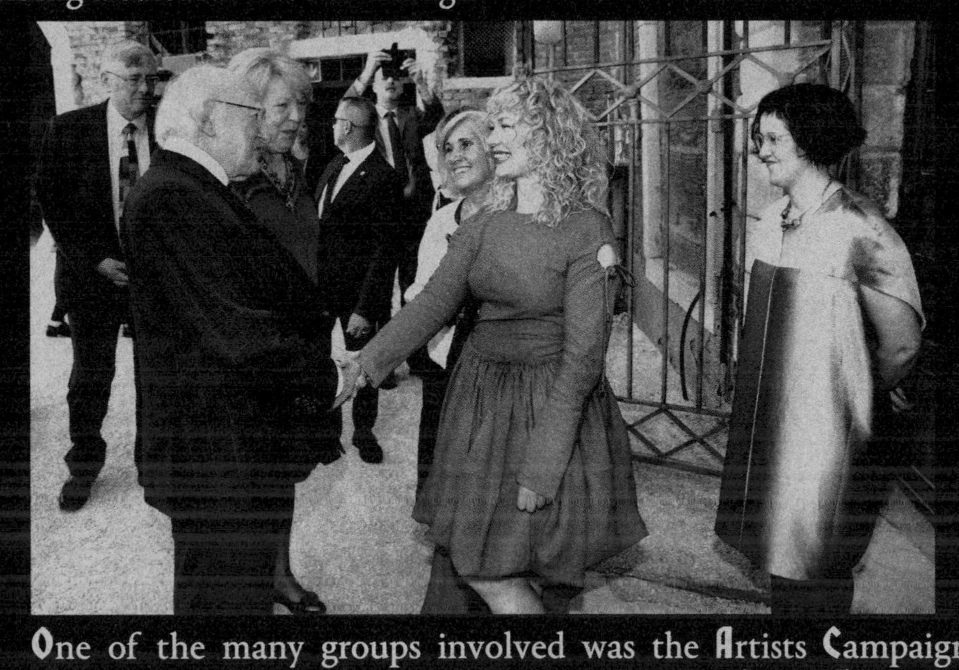

One of the many groups involved was the Artists Campaign to Repeal the Eighth Amendment, initiated by Cecily Brennan, Alice Maher, Eithne Jordan and Paula Meehan. This was reinforced by the marching banners, carrying rallying icons, made by Alice Maher, Sarah Cullen, Rachel Fallon, Áine Phillips and Breda Maycock. These were artists as activists, channelling their messages unequivocally into the political arena.

*Tremble Tremble* was headed down another but not dissimilar path, one that would ignite on its international platform and implicate on a global scale, the politics of modern Ireland. When the artwork returned to Dublin only a week after the referendum was won, Ailbhe Smyth, who led the YES campaign, addressed the gathered audience and turned to Jesse Jones: 'It was like you knew, in witch-like fashion, exactly what we needed to do and to hear and to see and to fear.'

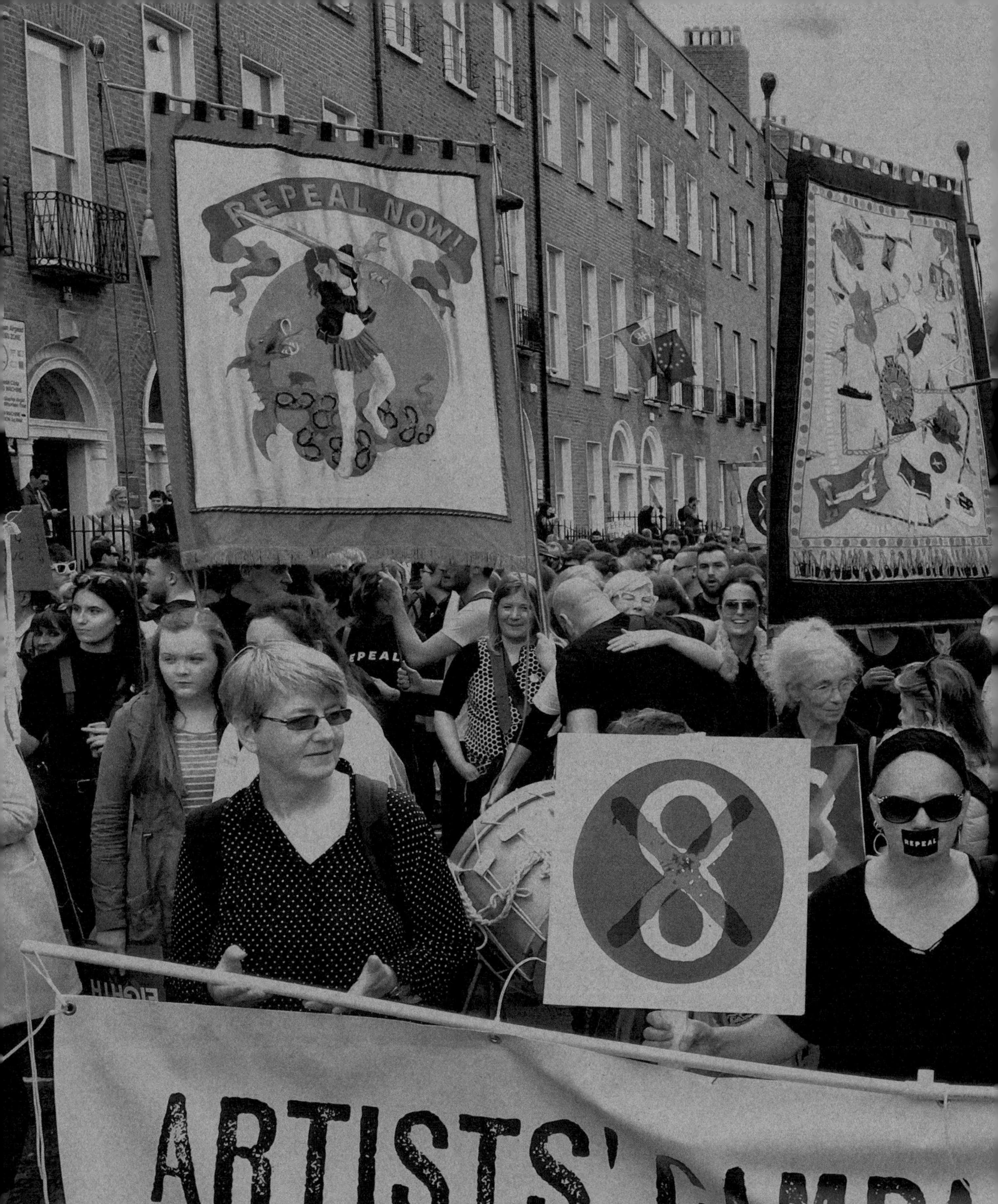
REPEAL NOW!
8
ARTISTS' CAMPA
TO REPEAL THE
EIGHTH AMENDM

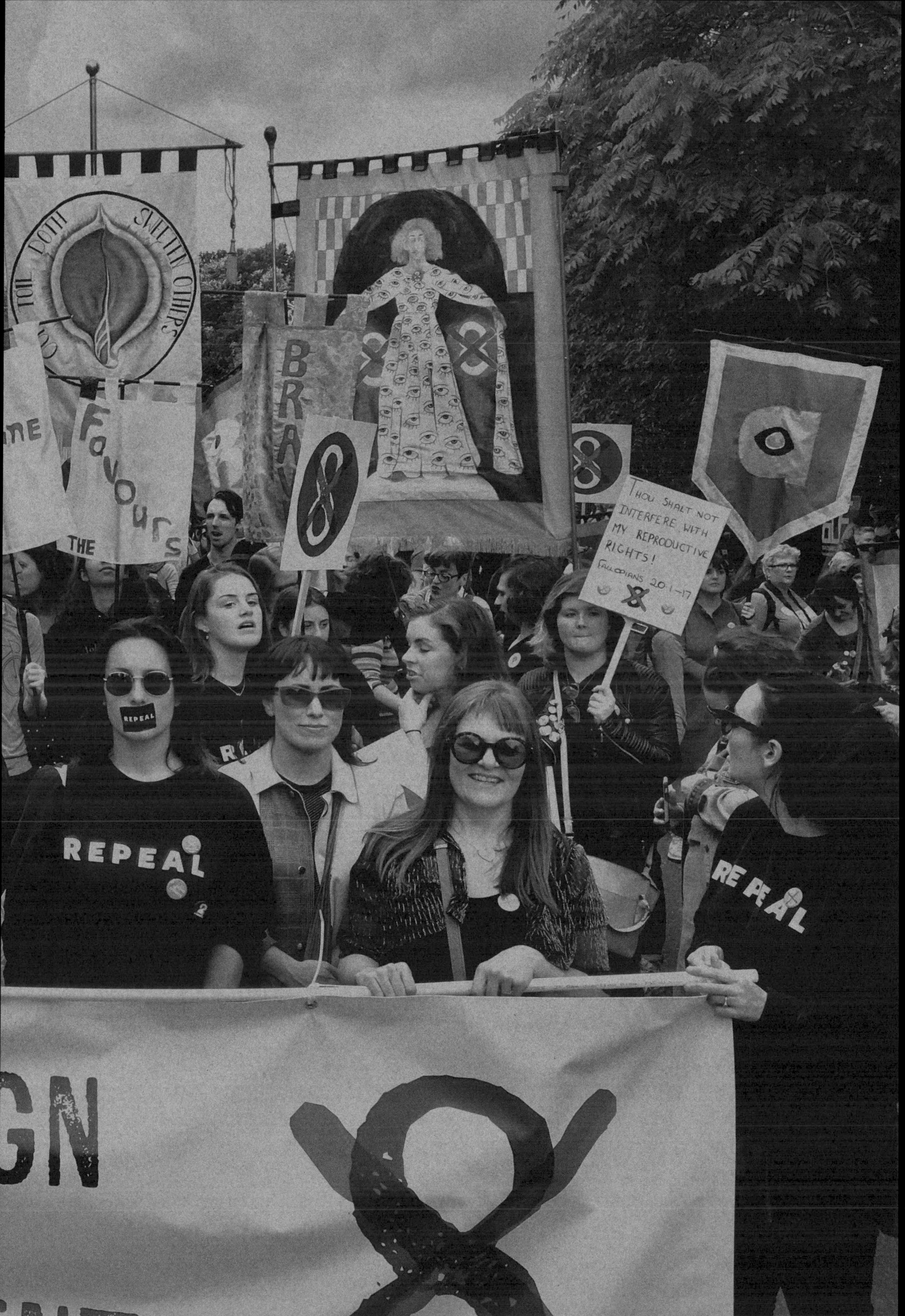

TOO LONG SHALL IN OTHERS
Favours
me
THE
BRAY
Thou shalt not
INTERFERE WITH
MY REPRODUCTIVE
RIGHTS!
FALLOPIANS 2:01-17
REPEAL
REPEAL
REPEAL
GN

Jones' artwork, which now lives in the collection of the Hugh Lane Gallery, is a complex assemblage of sculptures, videos, sound and light cues, composition by Susan Stenger and performance, which evolved wherever it was shown. But for Venice, the locus of our story, there were gigantic bones made to resemble those of the ancient Celtic giantesses, based on scientific analysis of Lucy Australopithecus' bones (the oldest known hominid specimen); there was text read from the *Malleus Maleficarum* (1487), the 'hammer of the witches'; a former British magistrate's court as the set; the last words of Temperance Lloyd, burned at the stake in England in 1682; and enormous curtains printed with the embracing arms and hands of Olwen Fouéré. Fouéré's central film performance was intended to embody the giantesses of the past, the law, Lucy Australopithecus and 28 generations of women that Jones would say have survived the witch trials. And throughout the work, a proclamation of a new law – *In Utera Gigantae*: 'Be it ordained and enacted that the giant from which life emerges possesses a power to create and to destroy the life she carries.' It wasn't direct in its relationship to the Eighth Amendment, but it left audiences in no doubt that Ireland's contemporary conflict about the jurisdiction of the womb was part of the ancient battle over women's bodies.

When Jesse Jones gave her opening address in Venice, she recalled the life, and death, of Irish dentist Savita Halappanavar. Halappanavar died of sepsis following a miscarriage in a maternity hospital in Galway in 2012, as surgeons were unable to terminate the pregnancy and save her life due to the Eighth Amendment. It was clear that Jones' artwork was taking Ireland's national shame to the highest level of international cultural representation. *Tremble Tremble* was a beautiful artwork, mesmerising even, but it was intended to disturb.

A few weeks after the Biennale opened, I received the notification from Culture Ireland that the President of Ireland, Michael D. Higgins, had accepted my invitation to visit the pavilion. I wish I had kept the note, but it read something like this: The President will visit the Pavilion of Ireland at the Venice Biennale, and afterwards continue on to visit the Pope in Rome.

This was a President who wasn't constitutionally allowed to comment on what was becoming an inevitable drive towards

having a referendum. But his position on the issue was clear in
1983, and the media made no subtlety of the choice of route as he
made his way to the Vatican a few months later. This will forever
live in my mind as a piece of political theatre, concocted between
us, the President and the media – although never a word was
whispered. We invited Michael D. Higgins, he responded, and the
media told the story. But this story was beamed into millions of
homes, departure lounges and gyms all over Ireland, flicking from
images of Jesse Jones' 'strident, feminist artwork', to images of
the President in conversation with the Pope, leaving the public to
imagine what that conversation was all about. President Higgins
is much loved – he's a poet, a philosopher and a socialist – but
he is a powerful, thoughtful and strategic politician too, with a
wonderful dosing of theatrical flair. Jesse Jones used the platform she had, we used the window of time we had, and he
created the international focus. It resulted in a set
of associations that drove directly into the heart of
Irish cultural identity.

Within 10 months of the opening of the Pavilion
the referendum date had been set, and when we finally brought
the work back to open in Dublin at the end of May 2018, the
Eighth Amendment was history. Borrowing from Ailbhe Smyth's
powerful address, 'you first have to disturb, you first have to
disrupt ... putting an end to decades and centuries of turmoil and
suffering and pain, and terror and dread and cruelty. And that we
certainly as women will never ever be quiet, ever again.'

Since then, *Tremble Tremble* has continued to do its work
and Jesse Jones has continued to elaborate and personalise
the artwork wherever it goes. From making *argizaiola* to ward
off nefarious spirits in Museo Guggenheim Bilbao, or burning
(in the spirit of the 'hungry ghost') a Bill from 1821 to abolish
Ireland's witchcraft and sorcery act of 1586 (effectively sending
medieval women the tools for their emancipation) in Singapore,
the artwork has continued to address the historic oppression of
women.

Knowing that the artwork joins the Hugh Lane collection
brings a great joy, as it is now intrinsically part of Ireland's story
of cultural change and will always be protected and cared for.
But writing this account in the weeks following the US Supreme

Court's overturning of Roe v. Wade provides a harrowing reminder that for every tumultuous and progressive story around the ongoing battle over women's bodies, somewhere in the world the tide will be turning in the opposite direction.

With artworks and exhibitions that create a platform for debate within the national conversation, timing matters. Context is everything. Public debate needs art and exhibition-making to contribute to it because it needs diversity, surprise, history, adversity, poetics and yes, activism. Artworks like *Tremble Tremble* and many others that advocate, inspire, empower and emote, can change the way we live, act and perceive ourselves. And are made by artists who know that their art is not separate from the world around them.

1.
Federici, S. (2014 [2004])
*Caliban and the Witch*, Brooklyn,
New York, Autonomedia, p. 75.

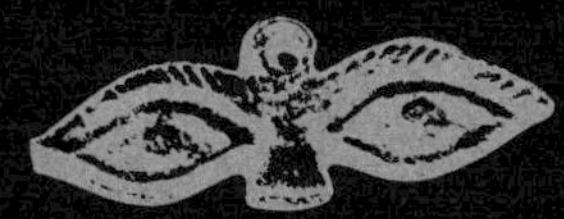

# The Tower

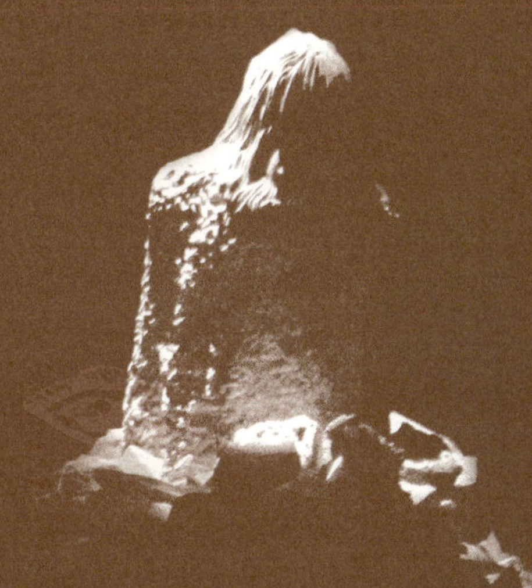

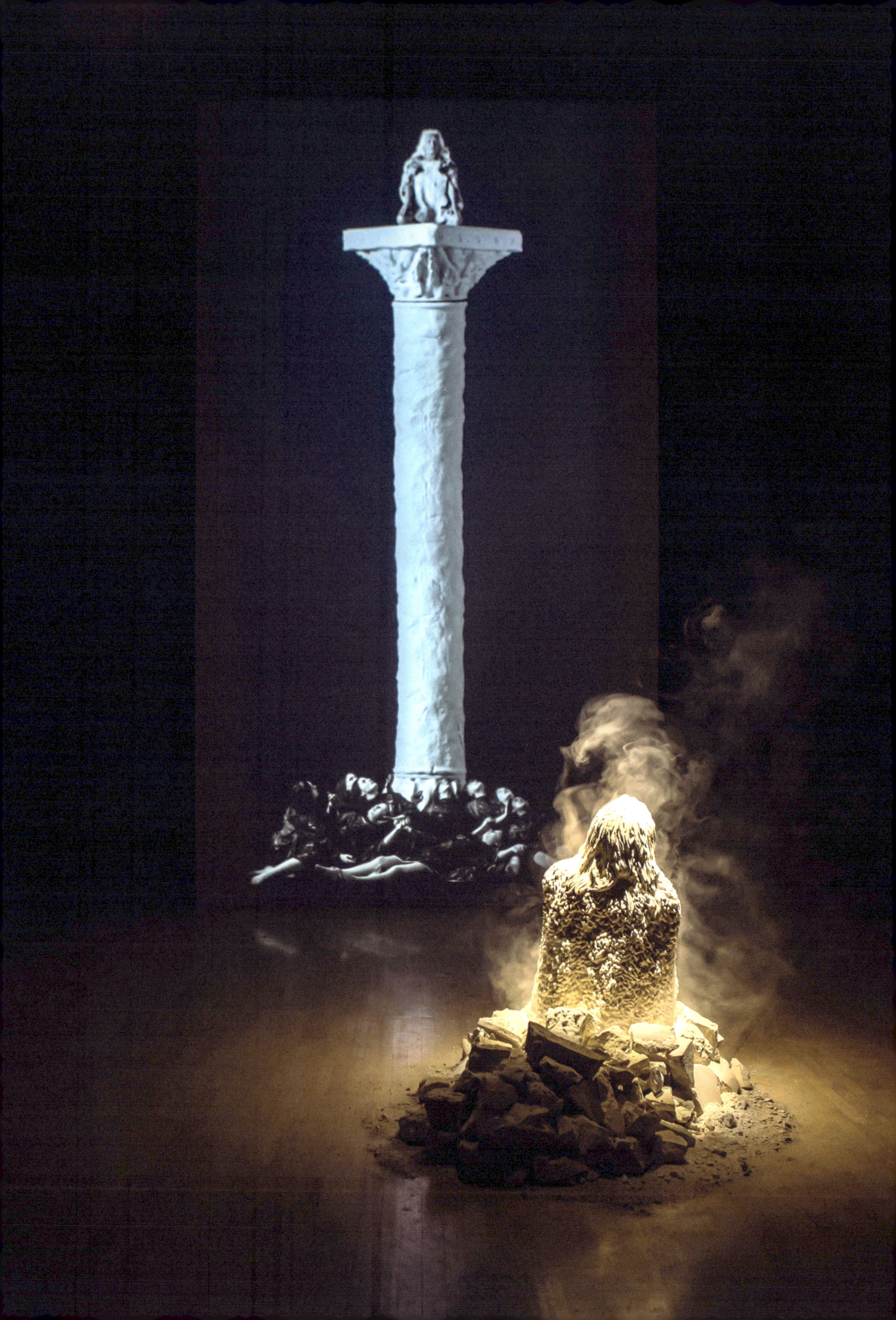

# The Tower

Tara Londi

Oh daughter, run because you were given wings
to fly by the powerful giver, who no one is
capable of resisting.
And so fly fast beyond all of these
adversities.

Saint Hildegard of Bingen

I in no way fear to gain the height.

Marguerite Porete

Jesse Jones' film installation *The Tower* (2022) does not revolve naively around the works of fourteenth-century mystical women. It orbits around them with such increasing speed that we too are scooped up, elevated into the higher, towering position of larger-than-life performer Olwen Fouéré, the statuesque Mary Magdalene.

Like a mobile vortex of rotating winds, the artist upheaves the long-occulted wisdom of eleventh-century German abbess Saint Hildegard of Bingen and thirteenth-century French Beguine Marguerite Porete to shed light on the period which anticipates the witches' inquisition of the following centuries.

From the intense mystical sophistication of their writings to the horror of their oppression and, as in the case of Marguerite Porete, public assassination in 1310, Jesse Jones gathers the symptomatic evidence of the frighteningly recent Magdalene laundries – religious institutions which, together with former workhouses, orphanages and industrial schools, formed the basis of the Irish State's treatment of unmarried mothers and their illegitimate 'issue' throughout most of the twentieth century (1926-1996).[1]

In *The Tower*, a chorus of 10 young women perform Saint Hildegard of Bingen's hymn *O Virtus Sapientiae* but again, as if caught up in the artist's invisible speed, the words twirl around. Their spelling is reversed. Their spell is restored.

Through Jesse Jones' artistic practice, a ritualised creation of magical counter-narratives, itself a counter-utterance, women's wisdom is thus reclaimed by the young women, their bodies re-sacralised, their spiritual life made whole again.

*The Tower* is a metabolic offspring of the horror, the abysmal depth, amplified, raised again in the acerbic lyricism of young women. Their vibrant density unfolds in the artist's speculative peripheries, shielded away from the 'architecture of confinement' where 57,000 babies came into the world and 'some' thousands of young mothers and children died, leaving no trace behind them. In their testimony, the surviving mothers tell of the 'unspeakable damage' that has been caused, and the children talk of 'lifelong feelings of isolation and abandonment'.

In *The Tower*, no detail is treated with the same dismissive neglect pervading these stories. The snaking hair of the girls' costumes is the exact dressing of Mary Magdalene's colossus figure. The fabric that makes them is infused with spikenard oil, traditionally used to prepare bodies for burial. Mary of Bethany massaged it on Jesus' feet before his crucifixion, intuitively predicting his fate, according to Catholic tradition.

As if spiked with fingers, the girls' hands become a syntax that guards the states of divine consciousness the Church refused them. Their movements map women's physical, mental and spiritual axes beyond the linear progression of religious history.

Their voice echoes deeper still inside the throat of prehistoric times, in the womb of time, and out of time altogether, where mystical experience evades historical narratives and sacredness is conceived as a potential for cosmic renewal. When venturing into spirituality and religion from the shanty towns of today's superimposed materialism and the ever stupefying, ever numbing digital world having hindered any potential education on the essence and gravity of the sensual or the sacred – one has to take an imaginative leap. The imaginative leap into fourteenth-century mysticism Jesse Jones brings forth with *The Tower* is a continuation of her research into how the 'law transmits memory between generations' and joins a feminist episte-mology that guards us against naive accounts of knowledge production and transmission.

First presented in 2017, *Tremble Tremble*[2] could be regarded as the first chapter of Jesse Jones' quest. Here the artist awakened the witches' voices, as an archetype for woman wisdom, their life emblematic of the persecution and historical omission whose legacy is all too pervasive today. As a follow up, *The Tower* presents two women, Saint Hildegard of Bingen and Marguerite Porete, who, despite a prolific literary production and in their own words, have warned us against the limitations of language. Their life experience is an archetype for women's collective wisdom, community living, interconnectedness across species, and the existence of life beyond the visible – a gospel for a feminist epistemology that precedes the plague of Reason of the centuries which followed.

Saint Hildegard of Bingen was a mystic, abbess, painter, poet, musician and healer, playwright and social critic. The fourth female Doctor of the Church, she composed a trilogy of visionary treatises (*Scivias, Liber Vitae Meritorum and Liber Divinorum Operum*). No other medieval woman, and few medieval men, achieved the level of Saint Hildegard of Bingen's literary and artistic production.[3]

Despite the three books, Saint Hildegard also translated the mysteries of life, which God entrusted her (visions and voices that came to her in broad daylight) through artistic forms: music, visual representations, and even the invention of a still undecipherable and unknown language, Lingua Ignota.

In *De operatione Dei*, Saint Hildegard brings together the three essential elements of a living cosmology. The first element is science: 'all science comes from God' and 'the greatest gift God has given us is our intellect'. In her books, Hildegard explores stones, rocks, trees, plants, birds, fish, animals, stars and winds, often anticipating laws of nature confirmed in the last century.

The second essential element is a healthy mysticism based on justice: 'singing justice in the hearts of men'. Justice for Saint Hildegard is the lived balance between man and the Earth. She is both a personal healer (writing about herbs and appropriate remedies for psychic and physical ailments) and a social healer: many of her sermons and letters deal with disease and social injustice issues.

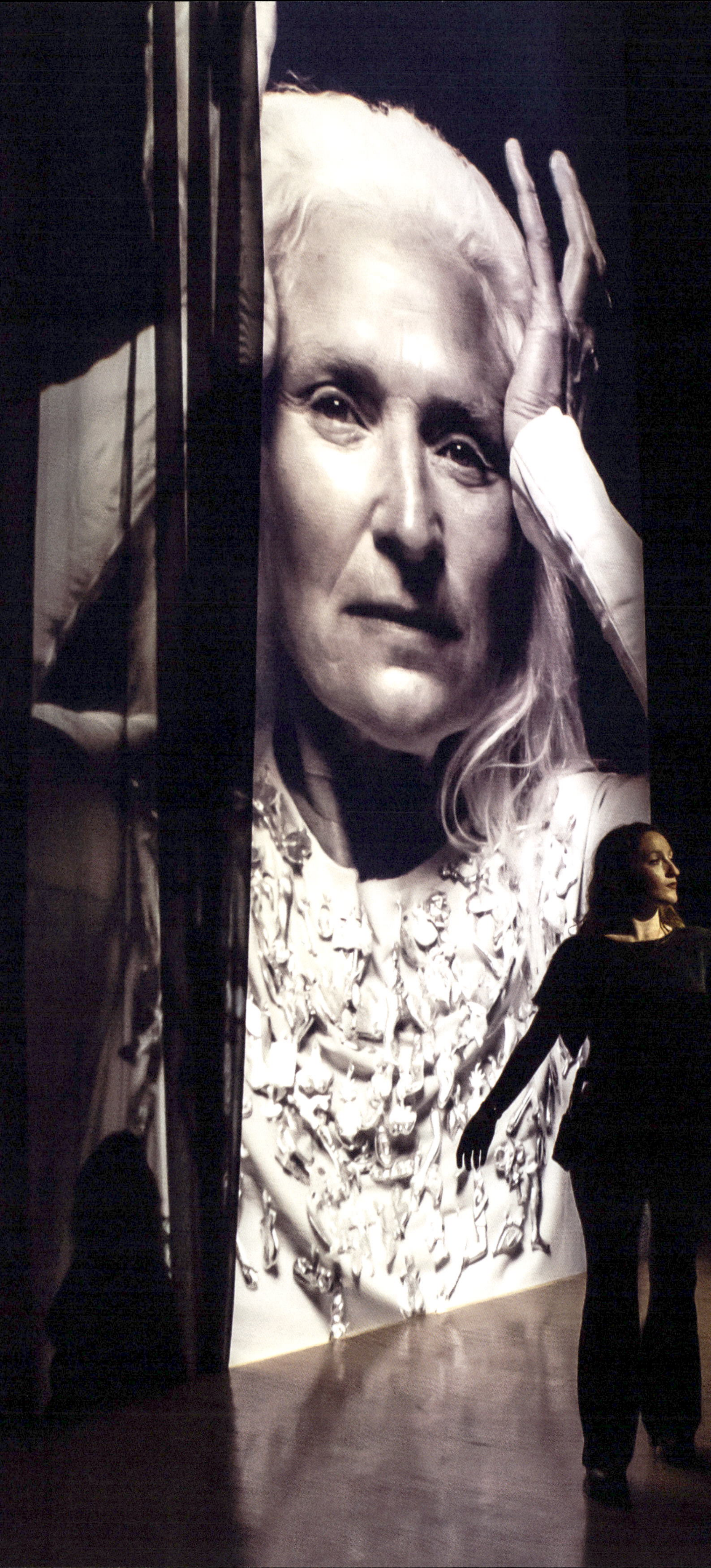

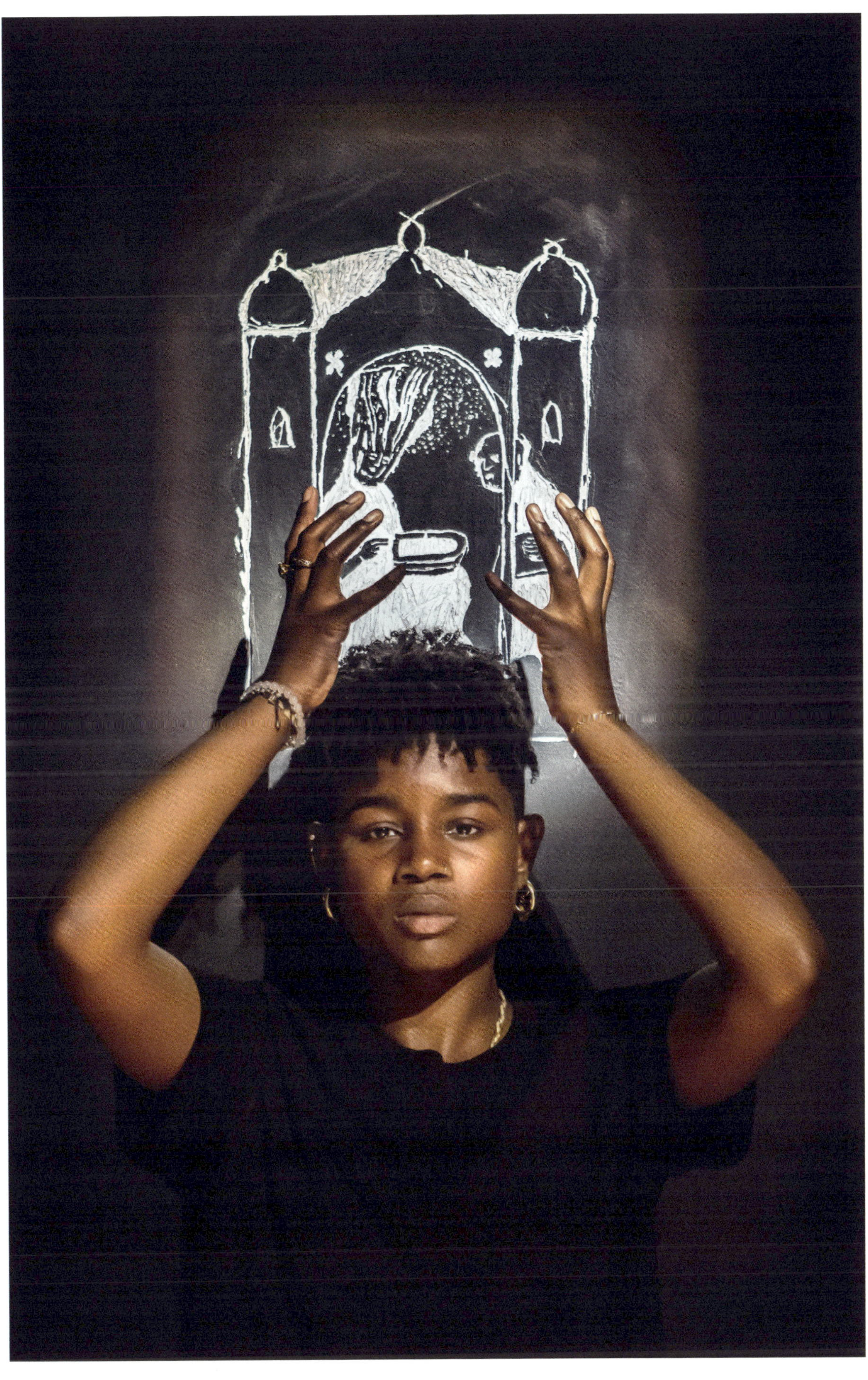

According to Saint Hildegard,
the third element of a living cosmology is art.

Hildegard of Bingen was forty-two when she wrote
*Scivias: Ways of Knowing.* Jesse Jones is the same age.

A great distance, in both time and geography, separates the German saint and the Irish artist, yet something of our earliest understanding of life colours both of their sensibilities: 'a primordial, a historical cosmic religion that was preserved since prehistory and that Ireland, being one of those European cultures shielded by the significant historical events, has succeeded in integrating into Christianity'.[4] If Jesse Jones has assimilated the flavours of the Celtic pagan wisdom she inherited by birthright, it is also interesting to note that Hildegard's life and formation played out in a pre-Christian spiritual site in Germany whose name, Disibodenberg, comes from Saint Disibode, one of the Celtic monks and missionaries from Scotland or Ireland who lived as a hermit on this mountain in the seventh century.

Hildegard's life (1098-1179), spanning four-fifths of the twelfth century, a time of effervescent creative and intellectual dynamism, contributed to the influx of female experience into Western mystical literature.

The spiritual awakening of this period was nevertheless different from others, marked as it was by a movement into the world, not a withdrawal from it. Marguerite Porete's mystical oeuvre, *The Mirror of Simple Souls* belongs to this tradition. Her vision of the soul in ecstatic union with God is a repetition of the Catholic doctrine of the beatific vision, albeit a beatific vision experienced in this life and not in the next.

Within this particular religious awakening, women galvanized themselves and developed forms of community life remarkable enough that one could identify them as a woman's movement.[5] The phenomenon of the Beguines is one of them, widespread all over medieval Europe. With men fighting and dying in the crusades and overflowing ecclesiastic institutions rejecting them, thousands of women joined Beguine institutions attracted by its emphasis on poverty, preaching and imitation of Christ and the flexibility and dynamism the Beguine life encouraged. The beguinages were semi-religious communities, and the Beguines worked, prayed, engaged with theological questions, bought and sold properties, maintained ties with their families and utilised their resources to aid their fellow Beguines and the communities. They could leave their order at any time.

Written sometime during the mid-1290s, Marguerite Porete's *The Mirror of Simple Souls Who Are Annihilated and Remain Only in Will and Desire of Love* is a treatise of some 60,000 words, written in vernacular French, as opposed to the customary Latin. Structured as a courtly dialogue between Love, Reason and the Soul, through a dialectic ballad of 87 chapters, Love attempts to explain to Reason how the Soul can become annihilated in God's Love. Love argues that once full of God's Love and united with God, 'The Soul transcends the contradictions of this world, but Reason, perplexed, complains that Love's teachings are full of confusing paradoxes ...'

The book was written to accompany other would-be 'simple' souls through the earliest stages of the spiritual life to its highest experience: the annihilation of the soul, its descent into a state of nothingness, and of union with God without distinction.

It is easy to see how Marguerite Porete's words, especially her belief that the simple soul should seek God only, for 'his teaching is not written down either in books or examples or in the teachings of men' attracted the ire of the ecclesiastic institutions. Marguerite goes as far as criticising the elite, because reason was what ruled 'holy Church the lesser', and by living by the counsel of reason, these clerics are 'stupid and asinine'. Because of their stupidity, she writes, she must 'be silent and ... circumspect in [her] words'. Marguerite was accused of heresy and was arrested in 1308. Throughout her trial, she refused to decant her views and was burnt at the stake in Place de Grève in Paris two years later on, the first of June 1310, holding her book with a solemnity that is said to have moved the public to tears. Her treatise would continue to circulate anonymously until it was finally recognised as hers in 1946.

In her book Marguerite Porete adopted the figure of Mary Magdalene to concretise the doctrine of the annihilated soul,

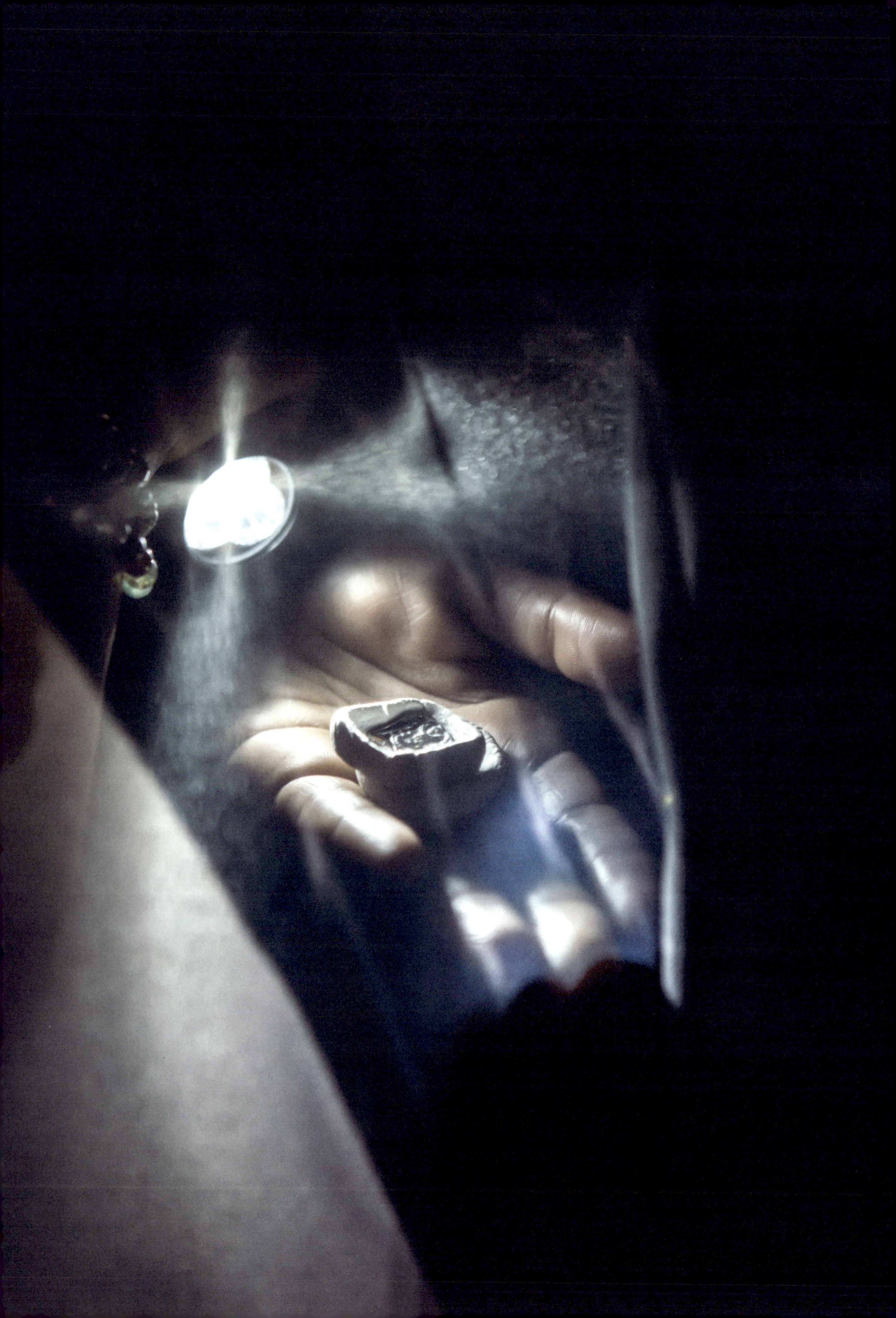

writing: 'she possessed so ardently, such work of goodness and she was so possessed by it and so strongly encumbered that the very encumbrance truly unencumbered her from herself'.

In *The Tower*, it is Mary Magdalene, her body adorned by Milagros,[6] that adopts Marguerite Porete's words in a game of mirrors, or *esprit de corps* (as is at times termed 'solidarity' in French: souls of bodies) between the two highly misunderstood women: 'Now listen, Reason, says Love, to understand better what you are asking about. A man who is on fire feels no cold, a man who is drowning knows no thirst. Now this Soul, says Love, is so burned in Love's fiery furnace that she has become very fire, so that she feels no fire, for in herself she is fire, through the power of Love which has changed her into the fire of Love.'[7]

Marguerite Porete's death was not only the murder of one singular woman but the condemnation of woman's mystical exercise. It tore apart the value of women's community and the moral standards that both Hildegard's abbey and the beguinages afforded and exemplified. It established an increasing depreciation of the Beguine movement and paved the way for the inquisitions.

With the decline of women's freedom of thought and expression, the masculine birth of the Renaissance imposed a cult of rationality. A certain and coherent knowledge of the world replaced the disorder of organic life, of nature, once alive and sacred, and gave way to the 'stability of mathematical laws and identities'.[8] René Descartes' *Discourse on the Method* defined a split between body and soul, and matter and energy, and his disdain for the body 'as separated' from the soul ('I am not this assembly of the members which one calls the human body') would provide further repudiation for women. Susan Bordo defines this time as a 'drama of parturition', regarding it as a tearing away from the organic and maternal universe of the Middle Ages to project oneself into a new world of 'clarity', detachment and objectivity. A 'flight away from the feminine, far from the memory of union with the material world and a rejection of all the values associated with it' is replaced by an obsession with distance and demarcation.[9]

At this delicate crossroad, humanity takes its turn, steering towards the era that we have come to know as the Anthropocene, or the Capitalocene. An era where among the many parables of imminent ecological destruction and extinction lies a fundamental paradox: the more human collective activities impact the environment the less the individual man feels connected to it. If human intellect appears to have an unlimited ability to invent and dominate, our bodies and sensations do not adapt as quickly to the pace of technological progress that our minds started. Our loss of contact with nature, our inexperience as part of nature, disinfected by the natural cycles of life, death and rebirth have left a profound trauma on human consciousness. Likewise, traditional liberalism's emphasis on individual freedom and emancipation risks excluding the idea of community as an essential component for human well-being, thus underestimating that we are what we are due to nature, culture and emotional ties.

Jesse Jones' practice resurrects ancient belief systems that have been bleached out from history and, by adopting collaborative methods and activating speculative worlds, questions existing knowledge systems: biology, ecology, geology and anthropology among others. Moving beyond the supremacy of the visual and the constraints of language, using immersive installations, Jesse Jones, like Isabelle Stengers,[10] argues for the continuation of the passion for truth, but through sciences that concern themselves less with the 'identification of possibilities' and more with what is not known or knowable.

The repercussions of the historical exclusion of women from the field of speech and the persecution faced by those who dared to organise themselves in communities reverberate to this day, but finding no words to articulate itself to reason, it is the howling that's left in Tuam, and it's sobbing that's left in Bessborough, and it's whining, and sobbing and weeping and bawling that we hear over and over from the mothers and babies institutions that will not be put to rest.

With gentle oscillations between mystic thought and the cosmology play of pagan rituals and symbolism, Jesse Jones nurses their stories like a midwife working through modes of vernacular knowledge and chaotic systems of elusiveness that dance chaos into harmony. A score emerges, with messy hair untangled by the hushed voices of the unheard, the disappeared and the forgotten.

1.
Willis, C. (2021) 'Architecture of Confinement',
*London Review of Books*, vol. 43, no. 10.

2.
*Tremble Tremble*, Jesse Jones, Irish Pavilion,
Venice Biennale, 2017.

3.
Hildegard's extensive contributions to Christian thought
are recognised in her being named as a Doctor of the
Church in October, 2012. Prior canonisation efforts that
began in the 1230s finally achieved their goal when Pope
Benedict XVI declared Hildegard's equivalent canonisation
on May 10, 2012. From Fox, M. (ed) (2012) *Hildegard of
Bingen, Book of Divine Works with Letters and Thoughts*,
Vermont, Inner Traditions – Bear & Company.

4.
Eliade, M. (1965)
*Le sacré et le profane*,
Paris, Éditions Gallimard.

5.
Stabler Miller, T. (2014) *The Beguines of Medieval Paris:
Gender, Patronage, and Spiritual Authority*, Philadelphia,
University of Pennsylvania Press.

6.
Milagros are small metal charms of devotional art.
Most are half an inch and are made up of many different
objects depicting body parts, farm animals, people
and more. Milagros are charms used for requests, for
protection and as a source of good luck. The word
'milagro' in Spanish means 'miracle' or 'surprise'. They are
typically pinned on wooden crosses, statues of saints,
the clothing of saints and other sacred objects.

7.
Porete, M. (1993) *The Mirror of the Simple Souls Who Are
Annihilated and Remain Only in Will and Desire of Love*
(trans. E. L. Babinsky), New Jersey, Paulist Press.

8.
Merchant, C. (1980) *The Death of Nature*,
London, Wildwood House.

9.
Bordo, S. (1987) *The Flight to Objectivity:
Essays on Cartesianism and Culture*,
Albany, State University of New York Press.

10.
Burrows, D. and O'Sullivan, S. (2019)
*Fictioning: The Myth-Functions of Contemporary Art and
Philosophy*, Edinburgh, Edinburgh University Press.

# The Void

Naomi Moonveld-Nkosi

IT IS OFTEN BROKEN THINGS WHICH HAVE THE GREATEST
OF BEAUTY FOR THEY KNOW OF LOVE AND LOSS.

STUCK IN A LIMBO THESE ANGELS DANCE,
NUMB TO THE PAIN OF REALITY.

GRACE IS GIFTED TO THOSE WHO HAVE SEEN
THE WANDERER OF PAIN AND HAVE SHOWN HIM PEACE.

WHAT IS LOVE?

IS IT INTERTWINED WITH HATE OR IS IT ITS OWN FORM?
THE SPACE BETWEEN HEAVEN AND HELL ISN'T AN IMAGE
OF ONE OR THE OTHER BUT A BALANCE OF EACH.

AS I GLANCE TO MY FELLOW SISTERS, I WONDER
HOW I FIT INTO THEIR LIGHT, THOUGH I AM THE ONLY ONE
WHO CAN SEE IT AND KNOW ITS NAME.

ENCAPSULATED INTO THE WORLD OF CHAOS HOW DELICATE
THE ORDER OF IT DANCES IN THE CIRCLE OF LIFE.

WHERE DO ALL THOSE LOST THINGS,
MEMORIES AND PEOPLE DISAPPEAR TO?

PERHAPS IT IS IN THIS VOID, THIS SPACE OF MYSTERY
WHERE I WANDER AIMLESSLY, TELLING STORIES OF
THE PAST, RUNNING FROM THE FUTURE.

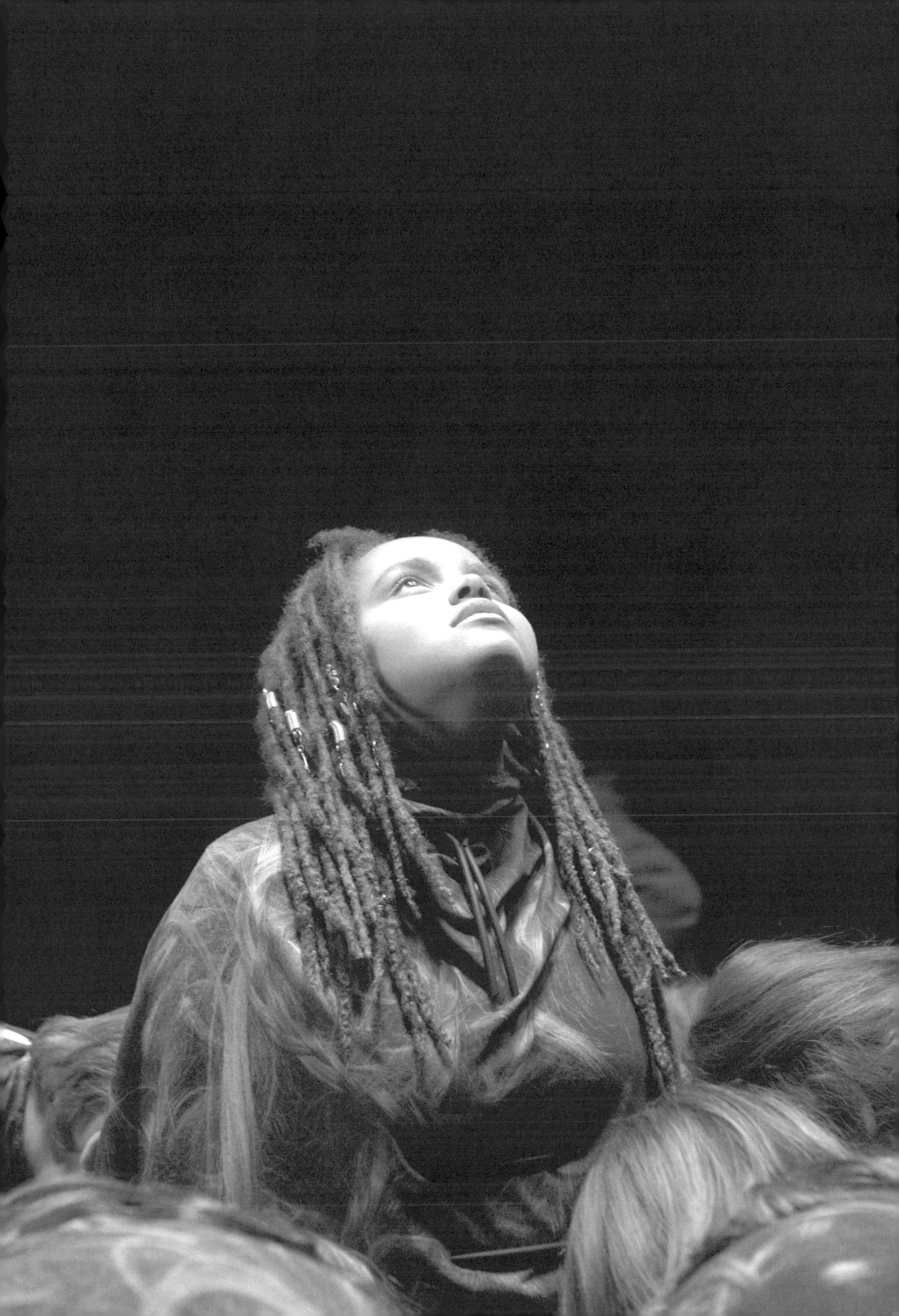

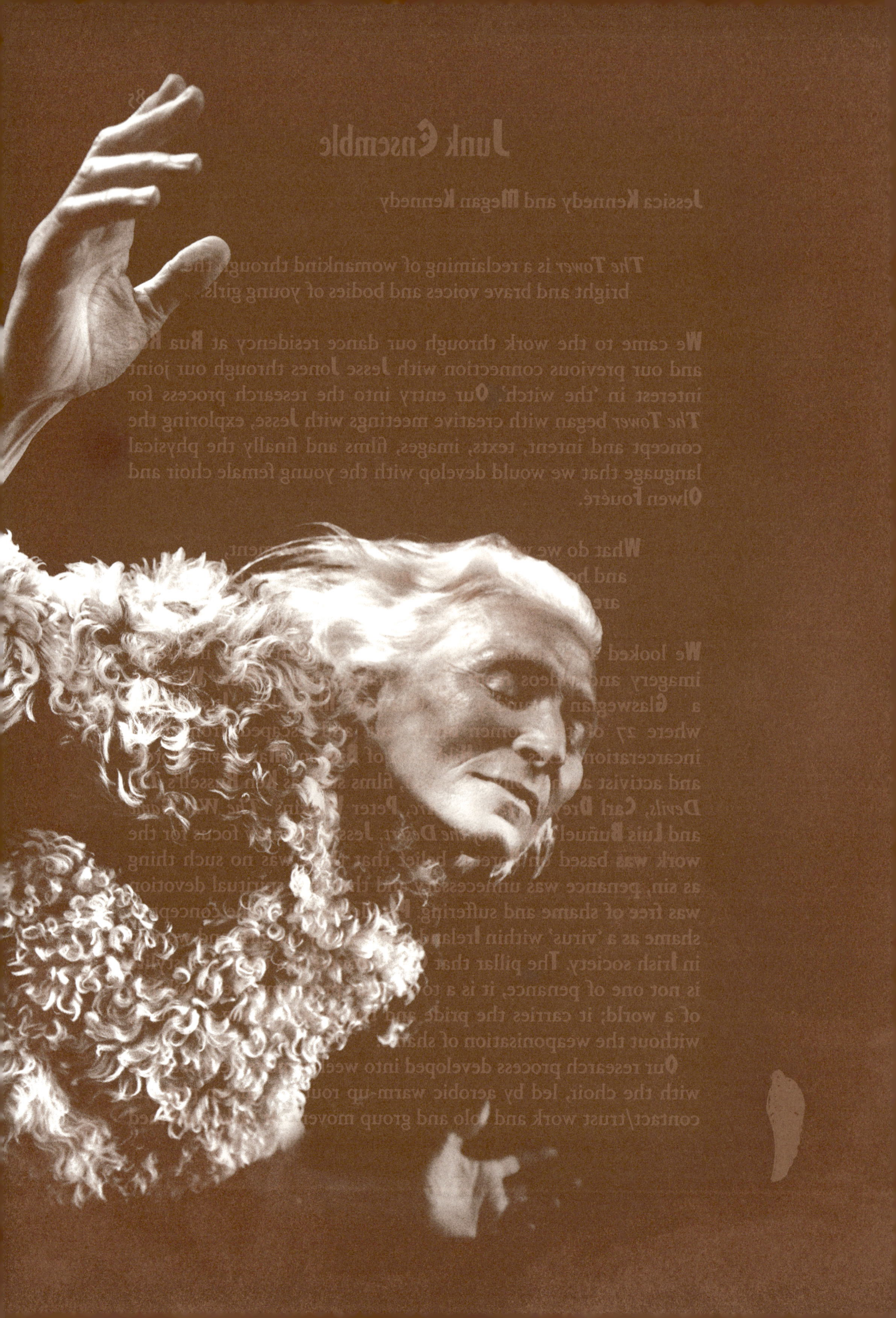

# Junk Ensemble

Jessica Kennedy and Megan Kennedy

The Tower is a reclaiming of womankind through the bright and brave voices and bodies of young girls.

We came to the work through our dance residency at Rua Red and our previous connection with Jesse Jones through joint interest in 'the witch'. Our entry into the research process for The Tower began with creative meetings with Jesse, exploring the concept and intent, texts, images, films and finally the physical language that we would develop with the young female choir and Olwen Fouéré.

What do we w[…] and bo[…] are[…]

We looked a[…] imagery and videos […] a Glaswegian […] where 27 of […] women […] incarceration […] and activist a[…] Devils, Carl Dreyer['s…] and Luis Buñuel['s…] work was based on the […] belief that there was no such thing as sin, penance was unne[cessary] and that […] spiritual devotion was free of shame and suf[fering]. But […] the concept of shame as a 'virus' within I[reland…] in Irish society. The pillar that […] is not one of penance, it is a to[…] of a world; it carries the pride and […] without the weaponisatio[n of sha…] Our research process de[veloped into] […] with the choir, led by ae[robic…] contact/trust work and […]

# Junk Ensemble

Jessica Kennedy and Megan Kennedy

> *The Tower* is a reclaiming of womankind through the
> bright and brave voices and bodies of young girls.

We came to the work through our dance residency at Rua Red
and our previous connection with Jesse Jones through our joint
interest in 'the witch'. Our entry into the research process for
*The Tower* began with creative meetings with Jesse, exploring the
concept and intent, texts, images, films and finally the physical
language that we would develop with the young female choir and
Olwen Fouéré.

> What do we want to say through the movement,
> and how will we understand what their bodies
> are saying?

We looked at a number of references with Jesse, including
imagery and videos from the dance pioneer Mary Wigman,
a Glaswegian laundry (Glasgow Magdalene Institution)
where 27 of the women broke out and escaped from their
incarceration, texts from Hildegard of Bingen, Marguerite Porete
and activist author Silvia Federici, films such as Ken Russell's *The
Devils*, Carl Dreyer's *Jeanne d'Arc*, Peter Watkins' *The War Game*
and Luis Buñuel's *Simon of the Desert*. Jesse's primary focus for the
work was based on Porete's belief that there was no such thing
as sin, penance was unnecessary and that true spiritual devotion
was free of shame and suffering. Paralleling this is the concept of
shame as a 'virus' within Ireland, particularly for girls and women
in Irish society. The pillar that Olwen Fouéré sits upon as a stylite
is not one of penance, it is a tower that proclaims the possibility
of a world; it carries the pride and the pain of being a woman,
without the weaponisation of shame.

Our research process developed into weekly movement sessions
with the choir, led by aerobic warm-up routines, group physical
contact/trust work and solo and group movement tasks informed

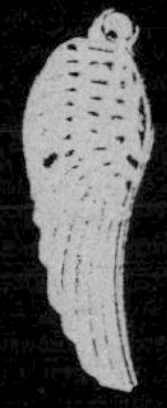

by specific text, imagery, montage, emotion and keywords. We split the choir into smaller groups and began devising around the themes of joy, shame, ecstasy, death; creating movement tableaus in response to these themes. We also explored bodies lifting, bodies falling, creating circles and moving backwards. This led us to the choreographic sections 'the nest' and 'the coven', whereby the choir began by lying on each other, a mound of bodies with their hair intertwined and limbs folded over one another. The women inhale and exhale together, breathing and living in one large nest or organism. This nest gradually rises to create a coven of bodies and a gentle swaying motion begins in the circle. Energy is passed through each of the bodies in a silent agreement, hair and heads touching and brushing off each other. The choreography of 'bodies lifting' came from the idea of weightlessness and the power/control of supporting one another, as the choir fully lifts three bodies into the air. There is a push and pull in the choreography as one body becomes helpless and needs support/lift to a higher state. Many of the choir members were unaccustomed to 'dancing', yet took to it brightly and unabashedly, and particularly shone when asked to create their own movement. Thus, the choir became creative collaborators in the project; their voices spoke and their bodies moved with an agency of their own. After three months of workshops with the choir, we refined the movement scores and expressions into specific sections for the shooting of the film, alongside Jesse. We worked with Olwen on her specific movement vocabulary, co-creating the physical language with Jesse and Olwen. Together we devised imagery that centred around fire, spitting words, communication/transmission, ecstatic movements and underside/flipping upside down, defying gravity, informed and inspired by a specific Marguerite Porete phrase. We continued to collaborate with Jesse during the film shoot, working on movement changes and additions to the shots. Seeing the finished film and immersive elements of *The Tower* in Rua Red's gallery was an affecting and powerful experience; the darkness of the space, the teenage girls' fierce spirit, and Olwen's aweing presence are evasive and enticing, demanding more than one viewing.

Our next collaboration with Jesse is for our upcoming work *The Witch Project // Powerful Trouble* in 2023. *Powerful Trouble* is an exploration and defence of 'the witch', pointing to the misogyny and cruel history of the witch and reclaiming the word in our society. Collaborating with a team of female Irish artists, we want to give shape, voice and form to 'the witch' and provide a unique platform to exchange and reframe these ideas. We feel this work is pertinent to the world we live in now and speaks to important issues such as equality, patriarchy and xenophobia. Our practice in dance-theatre is collaborative and cross-disciplinary; we often work with local communities and groups and visual artists in the creation and performance of our work. We have collaborated with two other artists from the *Magdalene Series* in our work: visual artist Alice Maher in the co-creation of a solo dance piece, *The Misunderstanding of Myrrha*, a retelling of a Greek myth and performance artist Amanda Coogan in *Dolores*, a reimagining of Nabokov's novel *Lolita*.

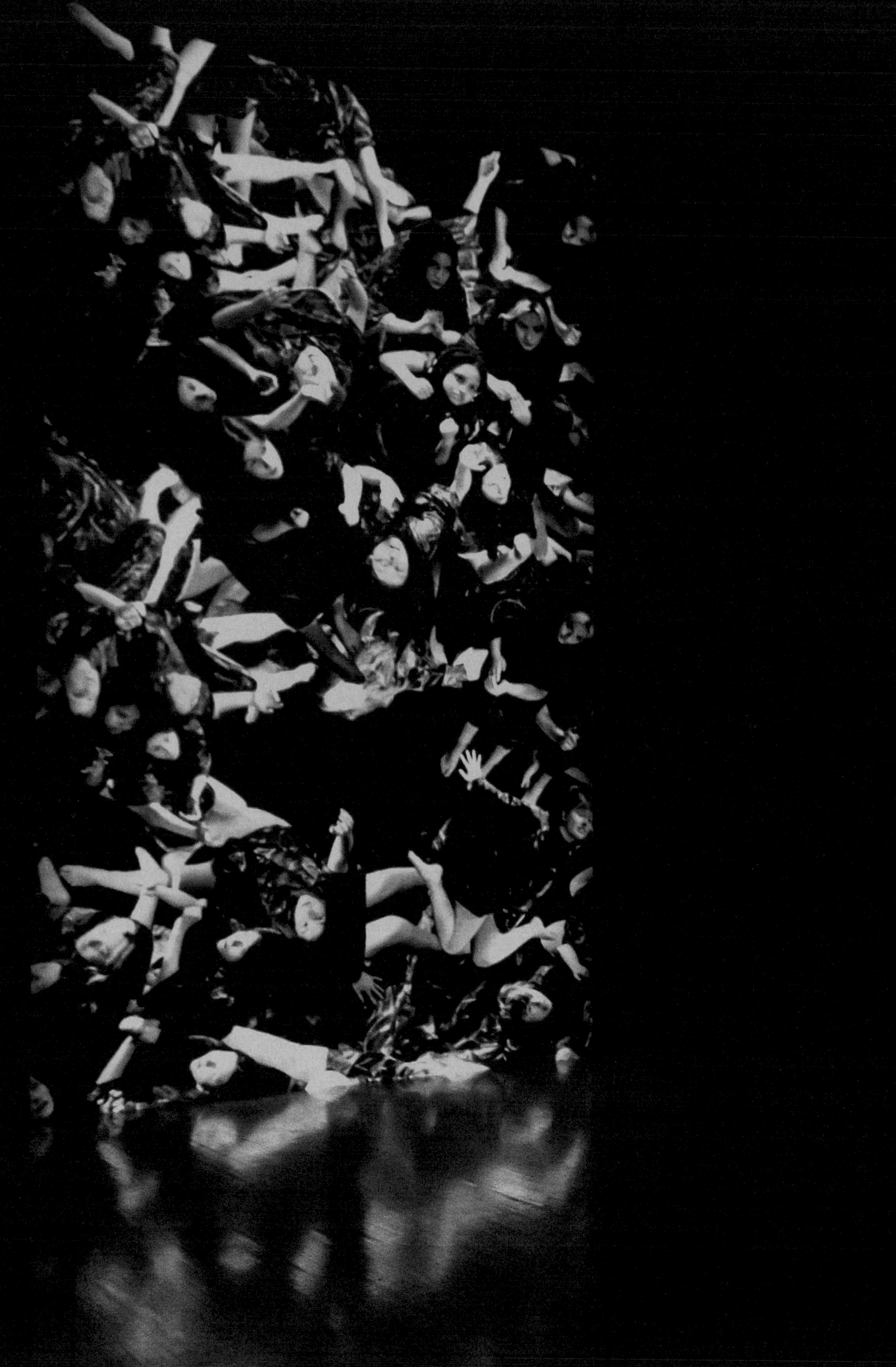

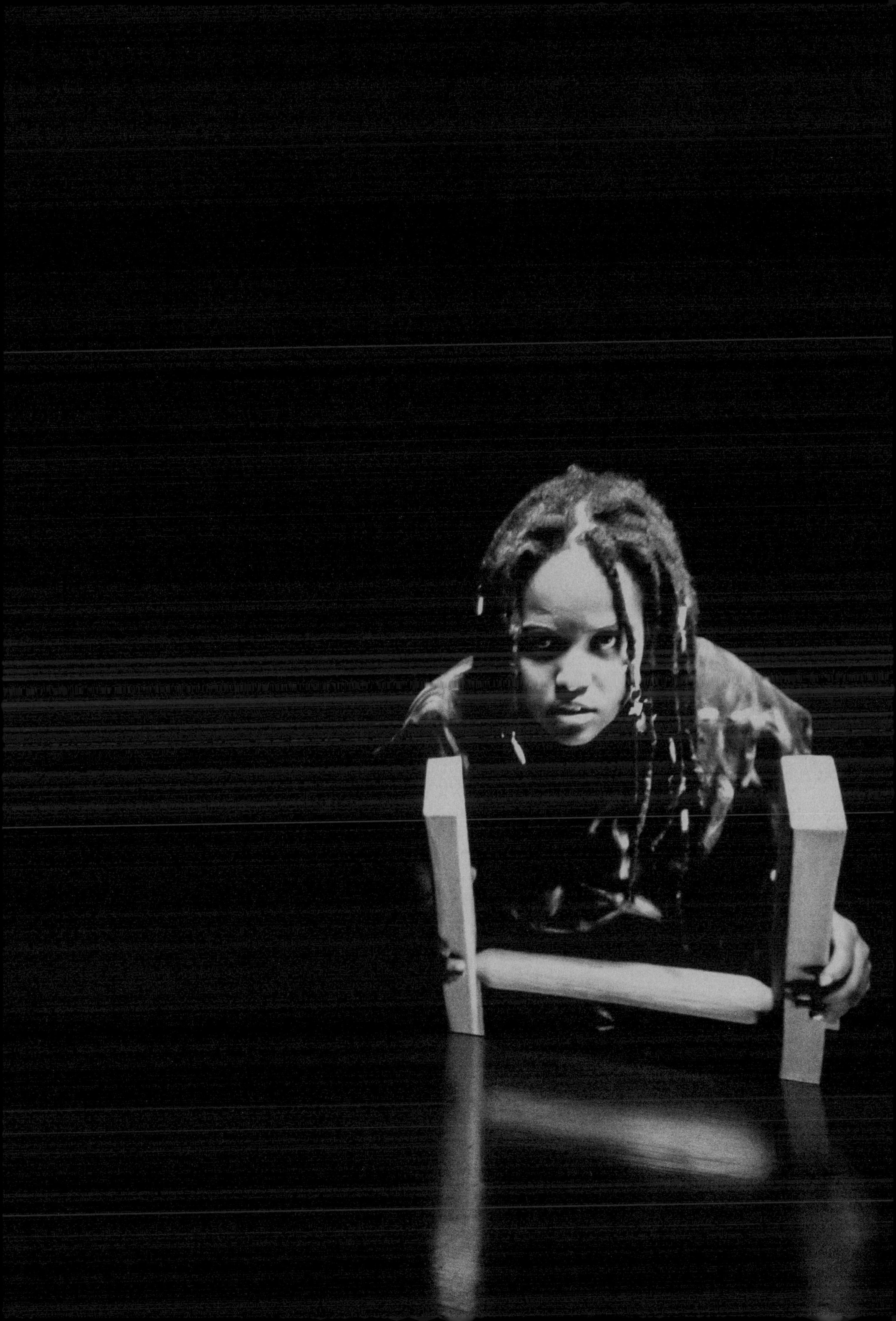

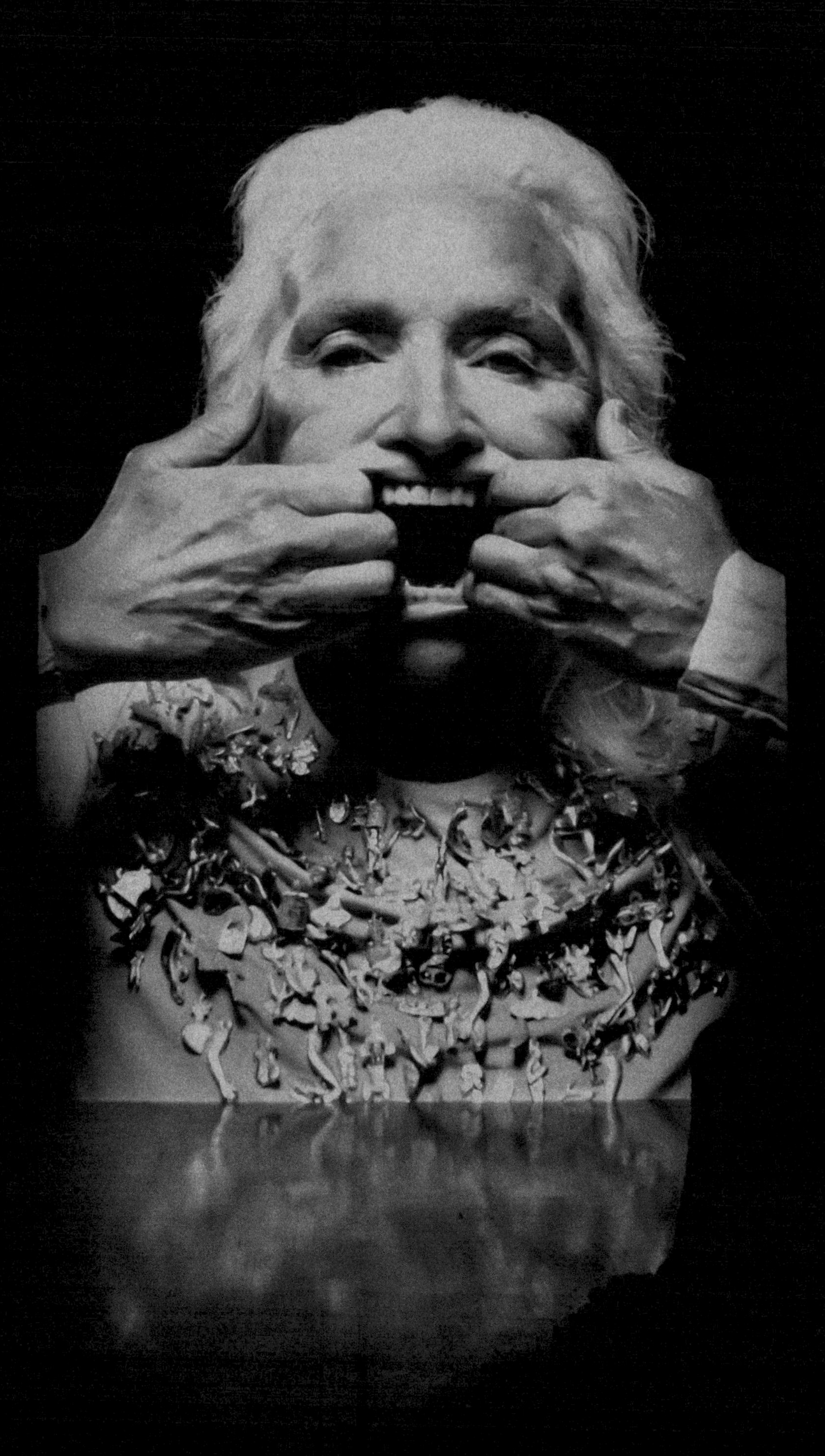

# Tessa Giblin in conversation
## with Jesse Jones

Much of the following conversation refers to the specific cultural and political history of Ireland and the United Kingdom. From 1983 to 2018, the Republic of Ireland's constitution included the Eighth Amendment, which equated the life of a foetus to the life of a pregnant woman – making abortion in Ireland illegal. This was added by referendum in 1983 and, after decades of campaigning, repealed by referendum in 2018. Prior to this, the Magdalene laundries and asylums operated in Ireland and the UK from the eighteenth to the late twentieth centuries. An estimated 30,000 women in Ireland alone were incarcerated for 'crimes' such as being an unmarried mother in these institutions, which were operated by religious communities and were quietly supported by the state. In 2013 after decades of lobbying, Ireland's Taoiseach issued a formal apology for 'the nation's shame'.

TG    If *Tremble Tremble* was influenced by the origin of the witch trials – why women had to be oppressed and their bodies controlled – *The Tower* takes us back two hundred years earlier to a time of medieval female mystics, decried as heretics. Could you describe this period, and who you were channelling as you prepared *The Tower*?

JJ    The spine of *Tremble Tremble* is Silvia Federici's *Caliban and the Witch*. In her opening chapter, 'All the World Needs a Jolt', Silvia maps out the curtain opener of the witch trials – the prophecy, or warning call. She talks about the veracity of the female imagination and how communities of women in the twelfth and thirteenth century found a space of autonomy through devotional practices. I became interested in female mystics like Mechthild of Magdeburg, Julian of Norwich, Margery Kempe and of course, Marguerite Porete, women who were engaged in anchoritism or their own self-sustaining communities such as the Beguines.

Hildegard of Bingen was a very powerful abbess, original eco-feminist and composer. She had psychedelic and very strange mystical visions – *scivias* – in her early forties, and was able to stand up to power, patriarchy and authority. But the rise of accusations of heresy, particularly towards female mystics, became an attack on women's isolated autonomy and eventually turned into the misogyny tsunami that is the witch trials. Marguerite Porete, burned at the stake with her books strapped to her body, is key to this bridging between the women persecuted as heretics and those as witches.

It's fascinating to me that we've been told a story of feminism that goes in waves and begins with the suffragettes. I was told this all through my twenties, and yet this is chronologically wrong as well as incredibly Eurocentric. Finding other moments when women's imagination has had agency and authority, for me, as an artist has been really inspiring. I have been thinking of Hildegard of Bingen as living like a contemporary artist: setting up her own space, wanting to be able to produce and have autonomy. It's basically like running a large studio practice. There was a real sense of the ambition of the female imaginary.

**TG** There are elements of *The Tower* that feel very similar to *Tremble Tremble* and others that are wholly different. Olwen Fouéré performs and collaborates in both of the works. In *Tremble Tremble*, Olwen was a giantess, a witch, a sleeping Lucy Australopithecus, the instinctual character of the Id, and even a garbled mouthpiece for the *Malleus Maleficarum*. How would you characterise her performance in *The Tower*?

**JJ** In *The Tower*, Olwen and I were thinking of her role as a kind of spiritual mother – a Sheelagh-na-Gig, or totemic goddess from a pre-Christian era. Although she's not a witch in this, as she was in *Tremble Tremble*, when we sat down to develop the character, we looked at what would happen if the witch was the shadow, the dark feminine, the debased, the violently persecuted. In *The Tower* this dark feminine is reversed, she is Magda. Magda is the Aramaic (the language spoken by Jesus) word for 'tower'. One of the arguments as to why Mary Magdalene was called the 'tower' is that she was such a knowledgeable, spiritual

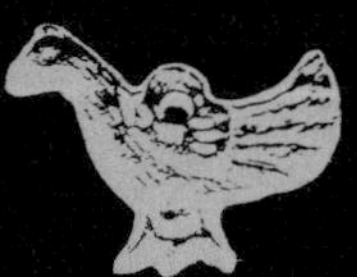

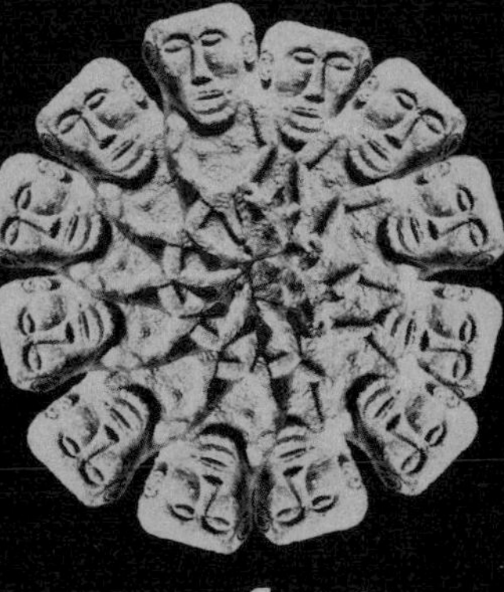

leader rather than because she was from the town of Magdala. Olwen performs this towering figure of Magda, who gives birth to all. She is the origin story that gives spirit to all the other iterations of the feminine that we see: the witch, the hag, the Cailleach (wise woman). She gives birth to all of these.

Another significant influence was Luis Buñuel's film from 1965, based on the story of Simon of Syria, called *Simon of the Desert*. It's a strange, surrealist story where Simon is on a pillar in the middle of the desert. He is subjected to temptation, often by a female character, who's trying to tempt him down from his spiritual piety on top of this pillar. I had been thinking a lot about the role of penitence, as a device for women. The penitent is, in a way, the opposite of the witch. She's apologetic. The public penitence of Simon of Syria and the male stylites of the period was not about incarceration and hiding, their shame was a public acknowledgment. They were put on display on top of pillars for the whole community to see whereas women penitents were hidden away.

We wanted to turn that imagery around, to turn that archetype around, where the penitent is transformed into this really powerful, totemic public figure that reverses the idea of shame. It goes back to the idea that Marguerite Porete had which was, 'If the sharp eye of the mind be turned towards nothingness, there can be no shame.' This was the most incendiary thing about Porete's book, *The Mirror of Simple Souls*, because basically she was saying – don't believe what the Church is telling you about sin and shame. What Olwen represents in *The Tower* is a prophetic figure who takes shame out of the picture. If we take away shame, we have a different connection with being in the world, and we have a different connection to understanding ourselves in relationship to power. And that for me, as a woman and feminist is so important to what we've experienced in Ireland over the last decade. It's been a huge moment of social transformation around shame and publicness, while at the same violence of what our emergent post-colonial state did to women through incarceratory shame.

I wanted to make something that would honour my own grandmother Rose, who was incarcerated in an industrial school in the early twentieth century. That darkness and violence is still there and has to be acknowledged. The figure of Olwen is like a breath of air that pushes it away and clears a space of thinking, of imagination.

**TG** As well as the Magdalene laundries, Ireland also had a history of industrial schools, one of which was the place your grandmother Rose survived – which you spoke about at the opening of *Tremble Tremble* in Dublin. Around the same time in 2018, women who had survived the Magdalene laundries were invited to give their testimony in Dublin, which you were asked to participate in.

**JJ** I was invited to take part in the Dublin Honours Magdalenes event at Mansion Hall in Dublin. I was a scribe for the day, working together with the survivors and a facilitator to gather testimonies for a permanent archive of the women's experiences. It was an intergenerational collaboration and what struck me as incredibly profound about the day was that women who were over 60 – most over 70 and some almost 80 – were talking about what had happened to them when they were 15 and 16. All of the really deeply moving conversations were based on their teenage memories – at a time when nobody listened. There was a sense of profound anger that these women, 50 years later in some cases, were talking about something incredibly traumatic that happened to them at the hands of the State and the church when they were 16-year-olds. There was a certain jubilance that an acknowledgment had finally come, but I remember feeling angry as well.

I began looking at parallel stories of Magdalene incarcerations, and I became really interested in the 1950s story of a group

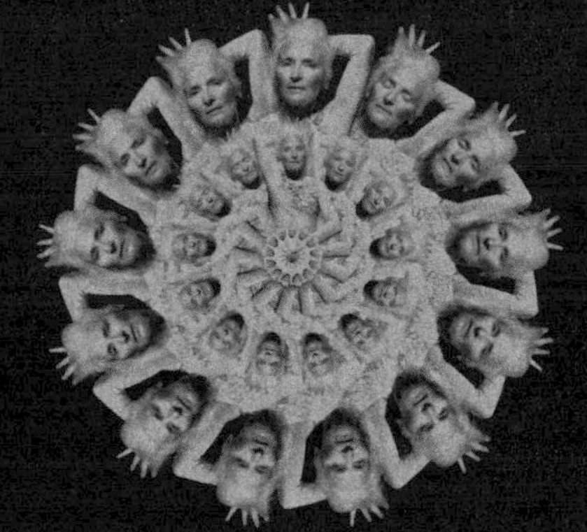

of teenage girls escaping from the Magdalene Institution in Maryhill, Glasgow. I went into the archives to look at the tabloid newspaper microfiche. It was a fascinating story, framed like a teenage 1950s delinquency narrative. But the story of the girls' escape, who were 15 and 16, was that when they ran away, they set up in an abandoned house, lit a fire, and were subsequently discovered two days later and brought back to the Magdalene Institution. When the press arrived, the girls dropped tiny pieces of paper with their testimony on it out the windows for the journalists to pick up. The girls managed to escape again, and when they did, they dispersed and disappeared back into Glasgow. The Maryhill girls were rebellious. I was fascinated by the teenage energy of that story. Ireland was a very different country in the 1950s because of our colonial past, with the Catholic Church's counter-revolutionary dominance of the mind and the body of the Irish. It was a completely different situation from Scotland.

When dealing with all these testimonies of the Magdalene laundries in Ireland, I wanted to bring this other experience of the 'what if' possibility. What if the teenagers in Glasgow's Maryhill were the Magdalenes that we were talking about in Dublin? What if we were to channel their resistance? That's when I started working with a beautiful young teenage choir. The first day that I went to visit them, I brought a very simple image: a photograph taken by Charlotte Rudolph that documents a piece of Mary Wigman choreography, where the girls are gripping their hands together so that it becomes a rope, or an image of a spine. I told them that we were going to work with Hildegard of Bingen's piece of music *O Virtus Sapientiae* and develop a piece of choreography based on this image.

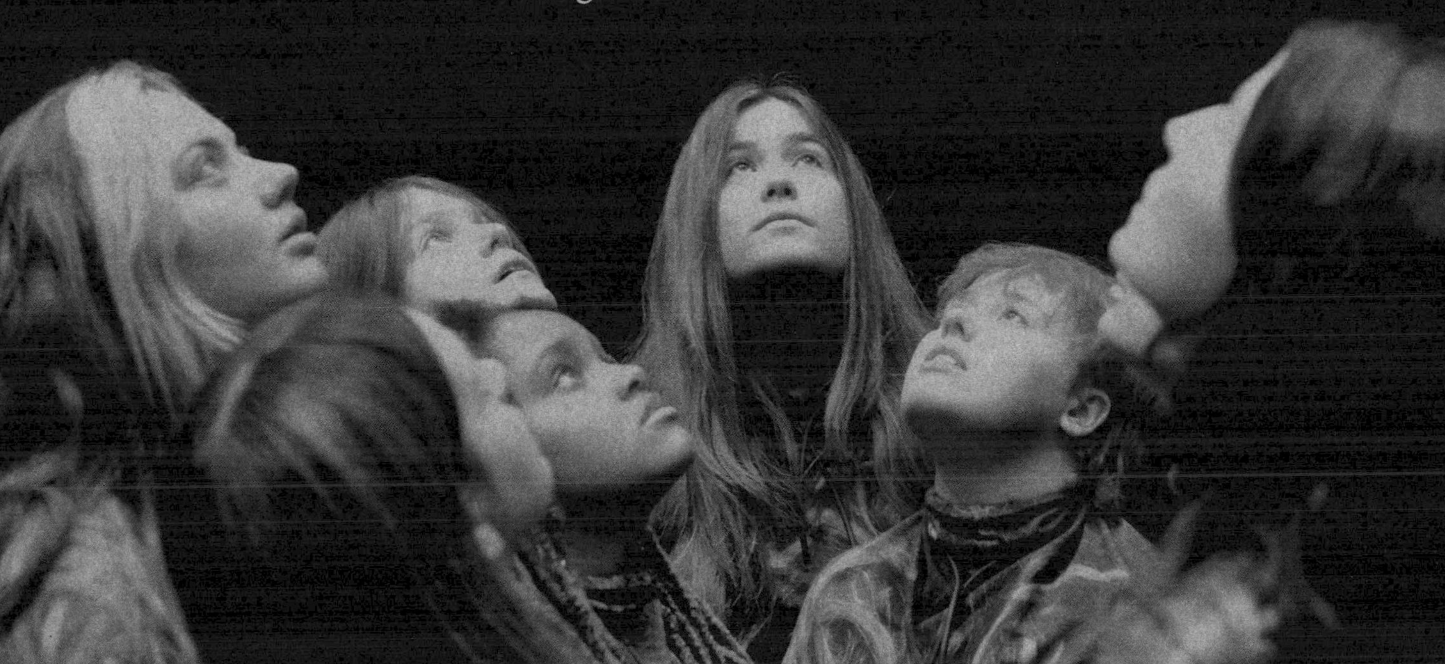

# Daily Record

**THURS SEPT 18 1958**

SCOTLAND'S NATIONAL NEWSPAPER

No. 19,620

1½d


# New uproar at Lochbu[rn]
# BREAK-OU[T]
# No. 2

## Girl smashes window and 27 rush out

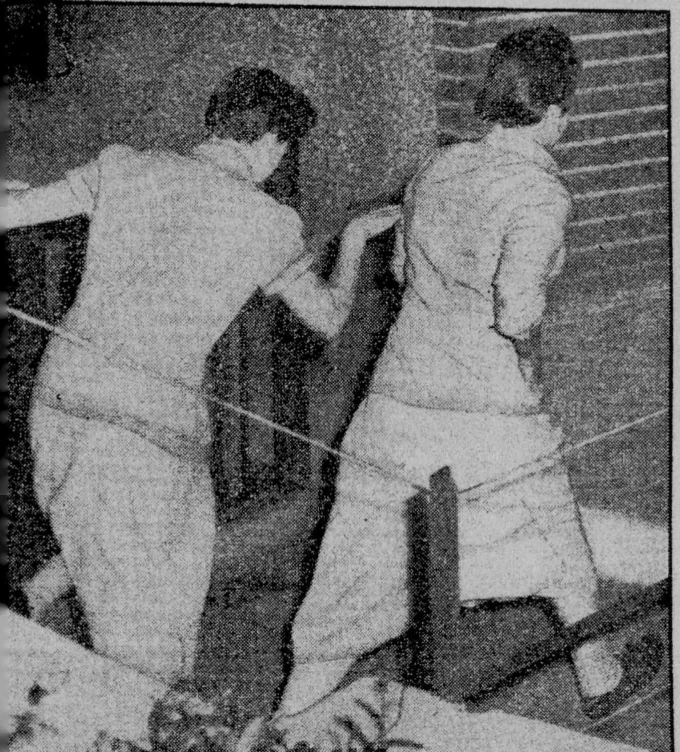

**This is how they went**

- Two girls (above) ran from the Lochburn home at Maryhill. Some of the escapees were caught before they left the ground, others were chased by policemen. RIGHT: The escape stairway.

THE GIRLS OF LOCH-BURN CORRECTIVE TRAINING HOME MADE ANOTHER FANTASTIC BREAK-OUT LAST NIGHT —THE SECOND IN 24 HOURS.

It was a sensational runaway . . . groups of the 'teenagers got away despite the elaborate security precautions clamped on the building after Tuesday's break-out.

Twenty-seven girls made a run for it just before 10 o'clock, an hour after they had been sent to bed and the home—on a hill overlooking Lochburn Road, Maryhill, Glasgow—plunged in darkness.

A crash of breaking glass shattered the stillness.

One of the girls, a towel wrapped round her hand, had smashed through an upper window leading to the fire escape.

They scrambled down the escape and ran yelling through the grounds, where 11 were captured.

Only a few hours before, Mr. Arthur Vaux, a director of the home, said:

"I don't anticipate any repeat of last night's trouble. The staff are on the alert and making regular checks."

Police cars patrolling the area converged on Lochburn Road where some of the girls had gathered in a corner of the grounds.

They were joined by Mr. John G. Leckie, another director of Lochburn, and for some minutes he talked to the girls over a fence.

### Scattered

He tried to persuade them to return, but they replied: "No, we're not going back. Thanks for all you have tried to do."

Then they disappeared, and a few minutes later were seen running down a side street.

They scattered in all directions . . .

Squad cars raced round the area, and gradually a few were rounded up.

Three walked up to a policeman on duty in Maryhill Road and said:

"We've come from the home. We want to give ourselves up."

Three more were brought back to the home in a police car . . .

Another was captured by a policeman in Vaila Street . . .

Continue[d]

● Mr. HANNAN, M.P.

"I'll phone the Scottish Secretary."

● ABOVE: T[he] outsid[e of the] home. BELO[W:] D. S. [M] chairman [of the] board of dire[ctors of] Lochburn[:] "I deny all [allega]tions," he sa[id].



## 3 a.m. FIGHT TO SAVE STABBED MAN'S LIFE . . .

DOCTORS early this morning were fighting to save the life of a young Glasgow man who was attacked and stabbed several times in the stomach.

And throughout the city police were warned to be on the lookout for a "tall man in a pale-blue suit."

### A description

The stabbed man, Robert McCourt, 25, of 59 Mordaunt Street, Dalmarnock, was seen staggering down Buchanan Street leaving a trail of blood.

A beat policeman ran over as McCourt turned into Argyle Street. Collapsing in the policeman's arms, McCourt gasped . . . "I've been stabbed."

He was able to give a rough description of his attacker.

An ambulance rushed him to the Royal Infirmary. At 3 a.m. he was still undergoing an emergency operation.

With stab wounds in the back, stomach and face, McCourt's condition was described as "critical."

Earlier in the evening, McCourt had been dancing with his young wife. Later he sent

**Continued on Back Page**

---

# Glasgow Magdalene Institution.

## INCORPORATED BY ROYAL CHARTER.

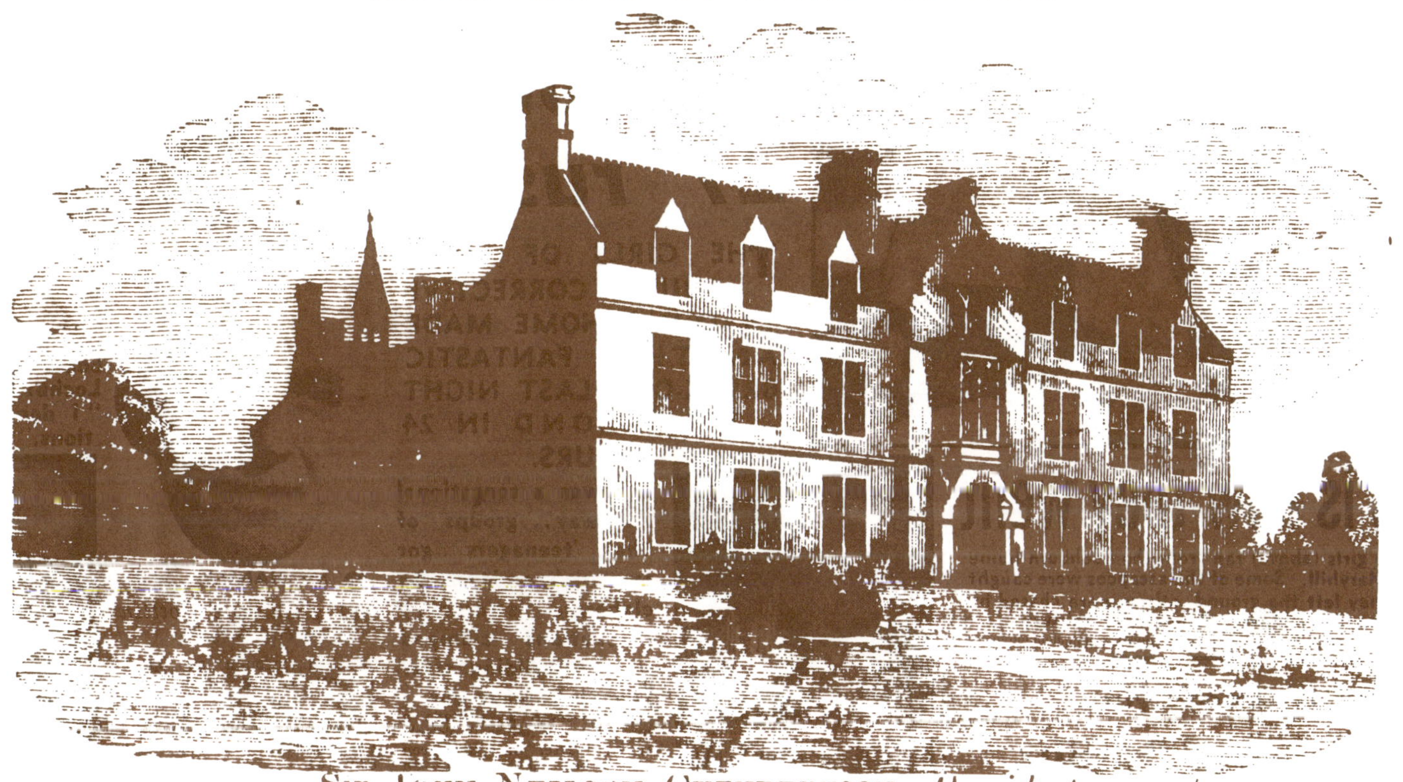

Sir John Neilson Cuthbertson, *President.*

J. D. Bryce, Esq.; Sir John Burns, Bart.; Jas. A. Campbell, Esq., M.P.;
Rev. Dr. Douglas; James S. Napier, Esq., *Vice-Presidents.*
Alexander Sloan, Esq., C.A., *Hon. Treasurer.*
R. W. Sinclair, *Secretary,* 15 Stirling Road.
*And a General Board of 42 Directors.*

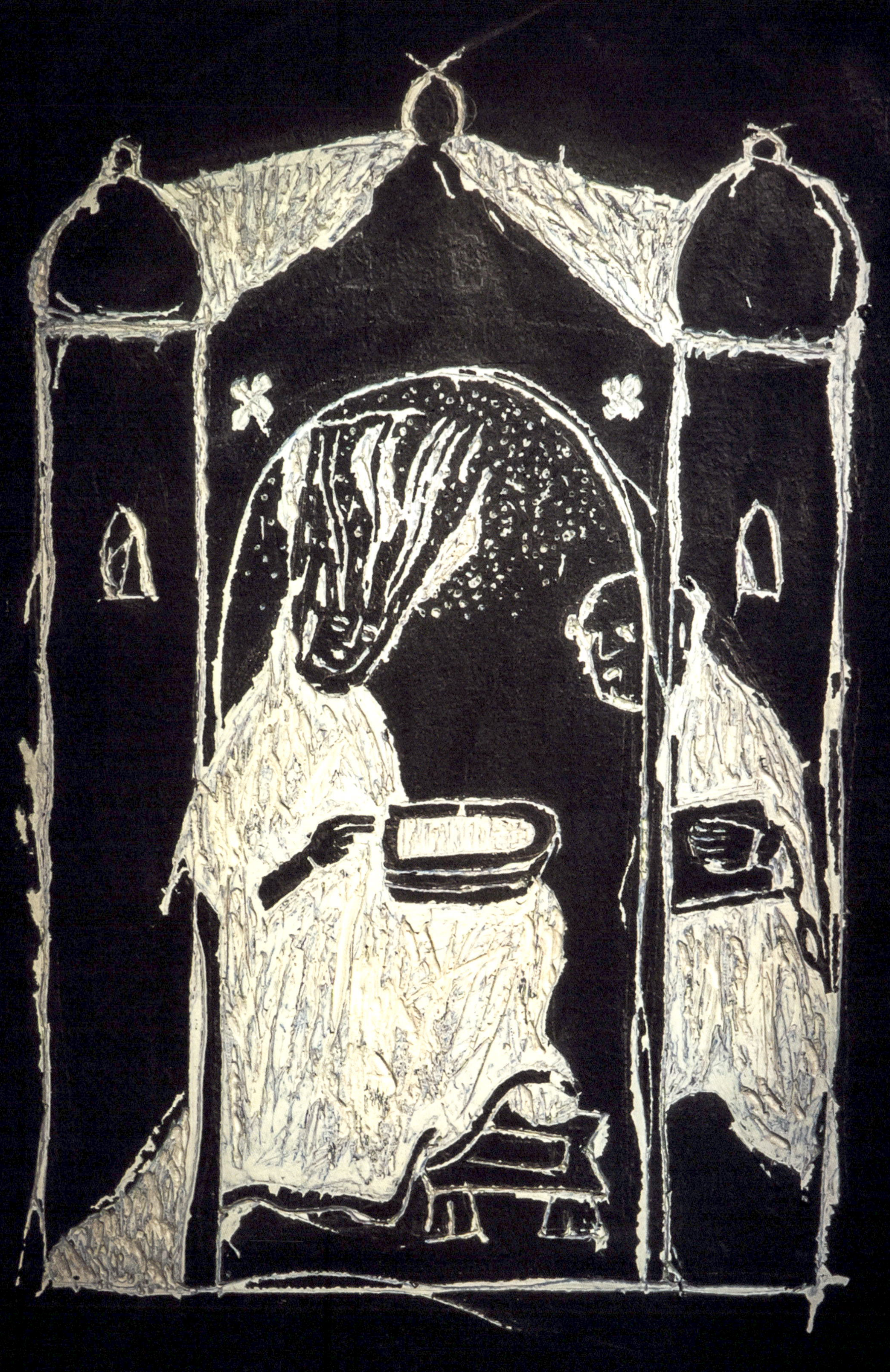

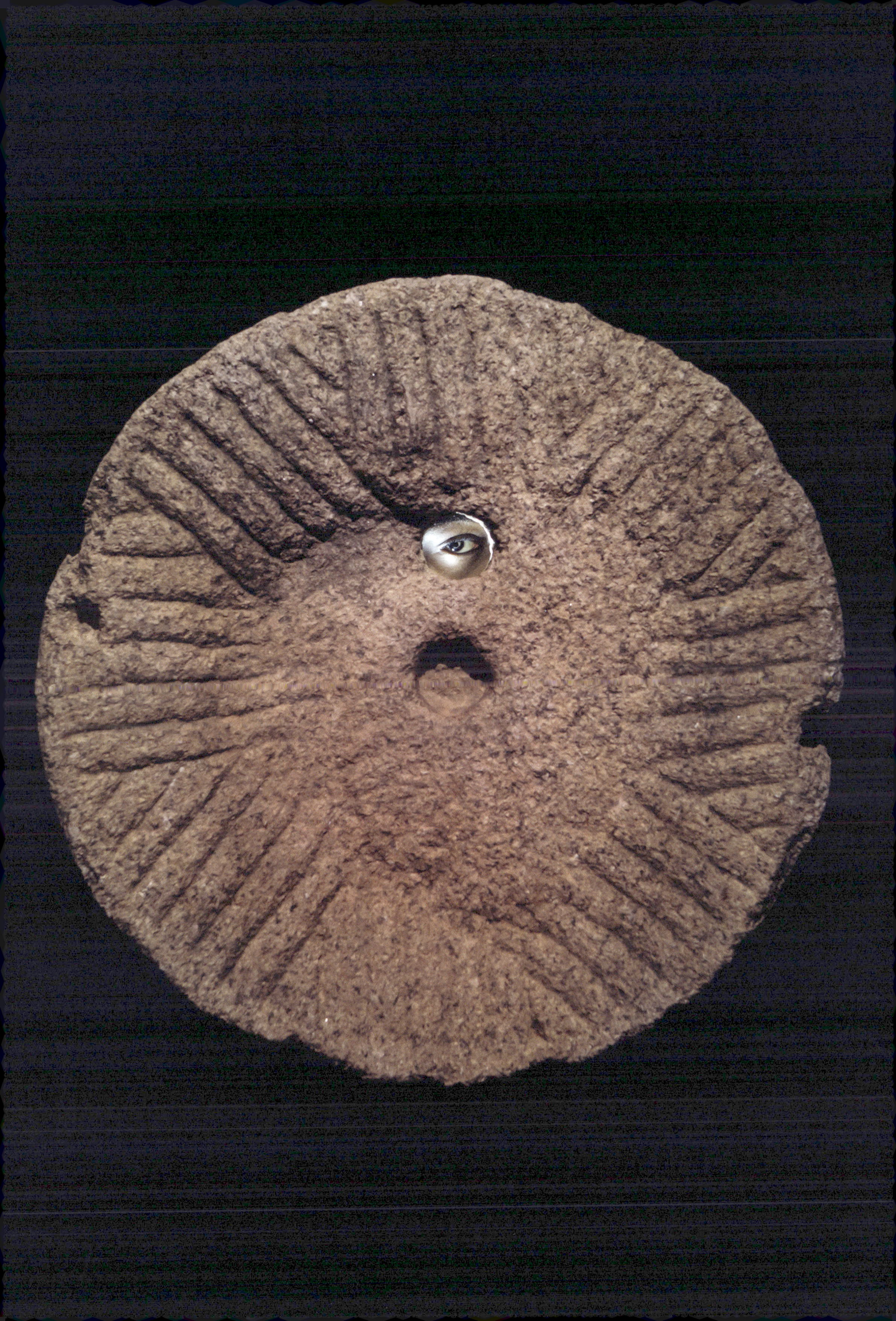

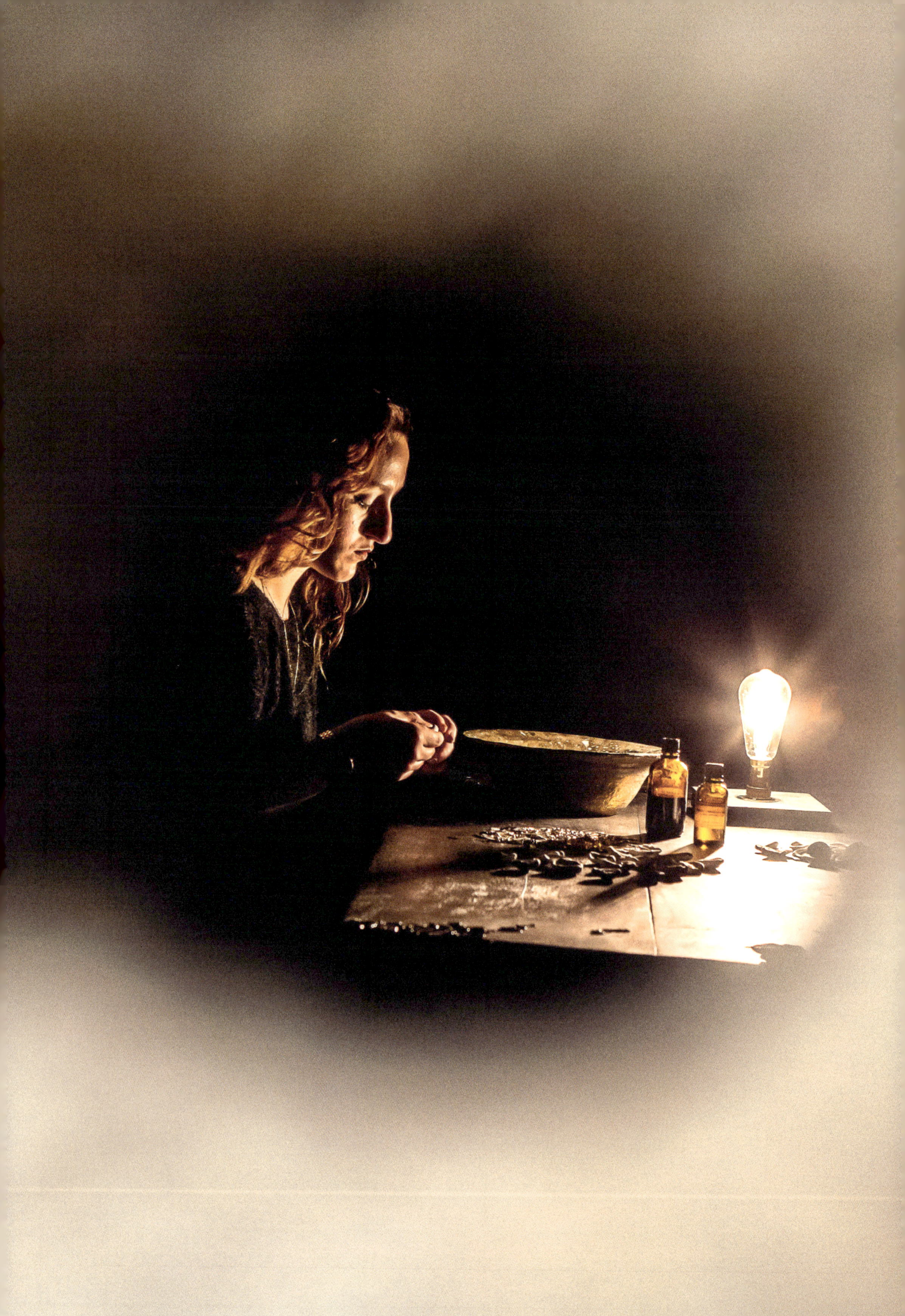

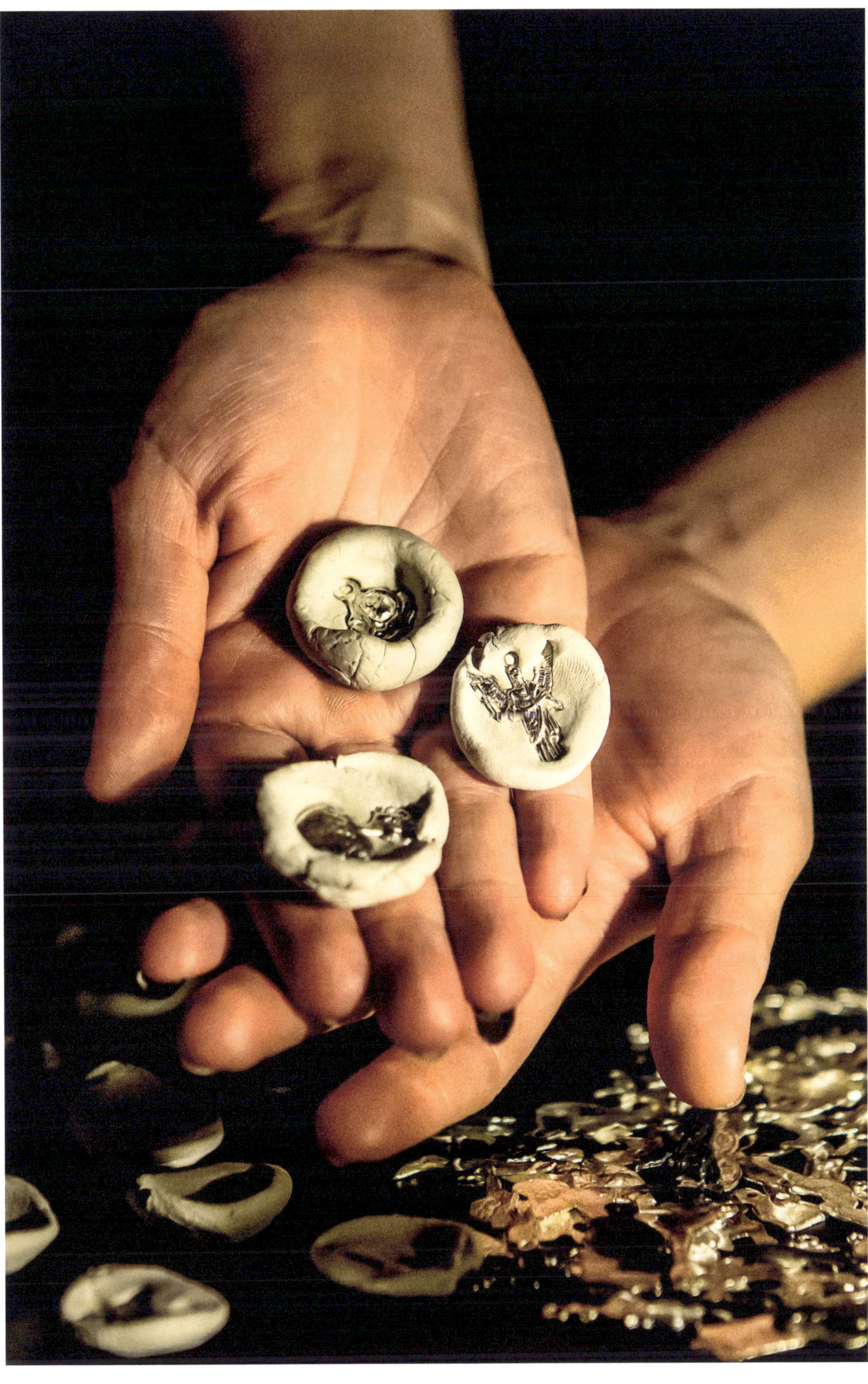

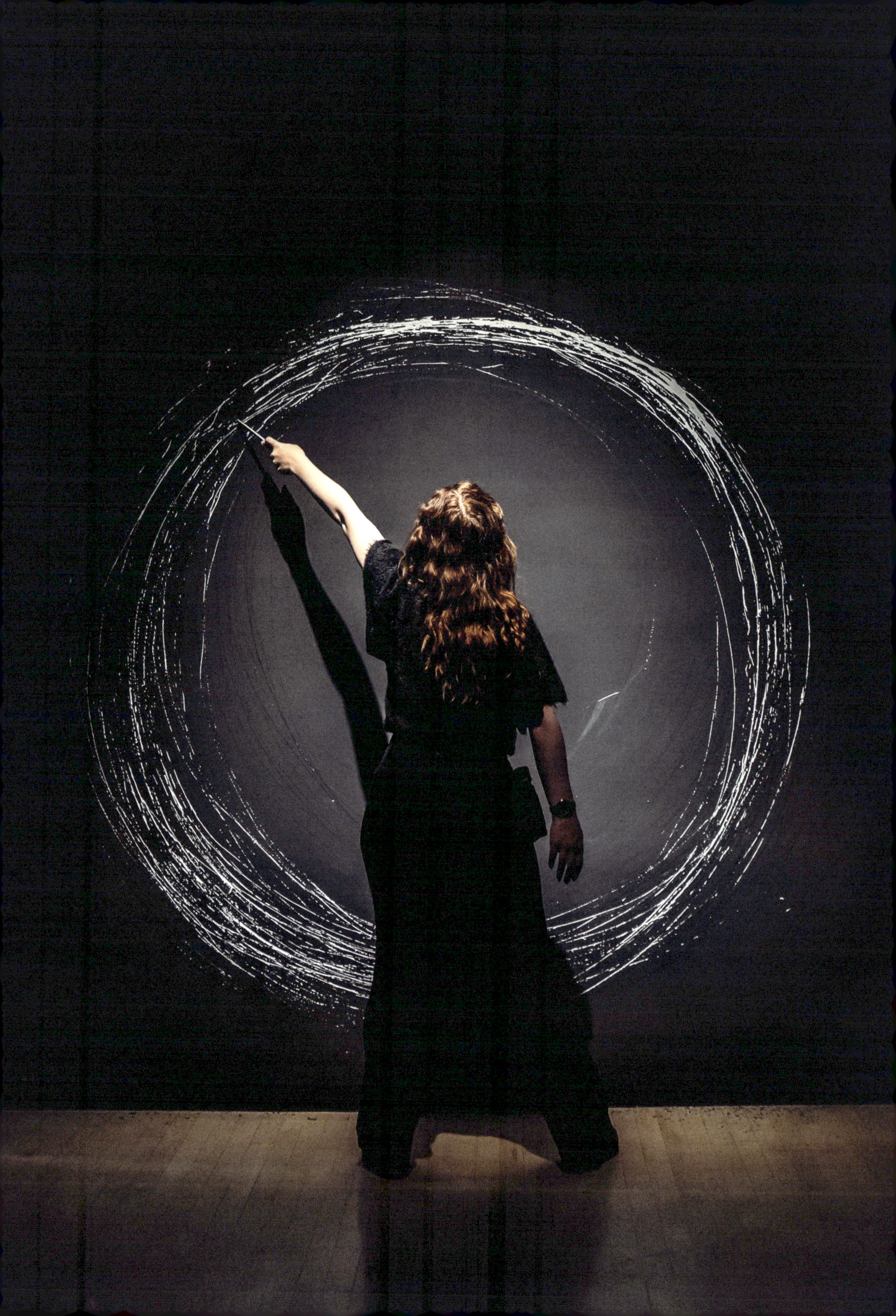

They weren't familiar with the Magdalene laundries, yet we were rehearsing a stone's throw from the Magdalene on Seán McDermott Street. The girls' movement really grew out of those conversations. I was also able to collaborate with Junk Ensemble as choreographers, who look to archetypes and history in mythology, signifying stories through the subtlety of the body incredibly intuitively, and as always there was a lot of Mary Wigman. She's always in the room.

In *The Tower* the girls' bodies are so connected they become like a nest. Naomi Moonveld-Nkosi, who plays the lead character, emerges from them as a voice that articulates the stories of Porete and the Hildegard of Bingen choral piece. You're not sure *what* energy is being brought into the room when you have a group of teenage girls, but the wisdom of working with young people is incredible. It was my first experience in a long time of working with teenagers, and we absorbed a lot from their own authentic way of interacting with each other.

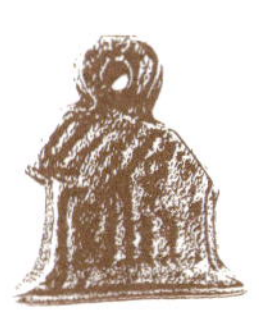

TG *Tremble Tremble* shares many formal features with *The Tower*. At what stage and for what reason did you decide you were going to re-open this research, this form, and make *The Tower*?

JJ *The Tower* really evolved from the 'task elements' of performance within *Tremble Tremble*, using objects and tools in one of its last iterations in Museo Guggenheim, Bilbao. One of the performers was carving a circle in the wall, first brought into the scenography as a clock – a way of measuring circulations or revolutions and thinking about time in a non-linear way. I was watching it and had a primal feeling that the performers were actually carving a portal; breaking down the wall between *Tremble Tremble* and what the next moment would be. Strangely enough the pandemic hit a week after closing the show in Bilbao. I went into an absolute cave during the pandemic's period of isolation, and continued reading about Mary Magdalene as a female archetype. I was reading about her in a cave in Provence where she spent 40 years being fed by the manna of angels, and started thinking about anchorites, who had long fascinated me. It was as though a portal was broken into *Tremble Tremble* through the use of those tools, and became *The Tower*.

TG  We're also introduced to elements of fire and burning from the beginning. The ladder installed within the space is deeply scorched, as is the worker's table.

JJ  The ladder from *The Tower* was connected to Marguerite Porete distinctively – a French mystic who was burnt at the stake in 1310 at Place de l'Hôtel-de-Ville, with copies of her book *The Mirror of Simple Souls* strapped to her body. In *The Tower*, Naomi Moonveld-Nkosi, who climbs the ladder, is playing the role of Marguerite Porete, as is Olwen Fouéré: both of their dialogue is drawn from her book. In representations of Porete you always see a ladder, a moment of ascension and destruction. It developed into a really significant, almost tarot card image in my head of a ladder on fire. These elements – the burned ladder, the burned table – they're burning with the intensity of the labour of making. In her book, Porete said 'I cannot be burnt', when she was talking about being attacked for heresy. 'I cannot be burnt because I'm already on fire with the fire of love.' This labour, this activity is what's happening at the table in Edinburgh.

TG  When *The Tower* comes to Edinburgh, this table is going to be housed in a 'cell' – an enclosed room. What compelled you to create this cell?

JJ  In Edinburgh, I wanted to drill back into those original moments of researching the space beyond *Tremble Tremble* – particularly because Talbot Rice is so far the one gallery to have shown both artworks. In the early days of the pandemic, I was reading a lot of Julian of Norwich, an anchorite (never leaving her rooms adjoining the church) and I became fascinated by what happens to the imaginary in isolation. I became drawn to the idea of creating a space, a secret, intimate space within the gallery where there's a troubling between being public and being private.

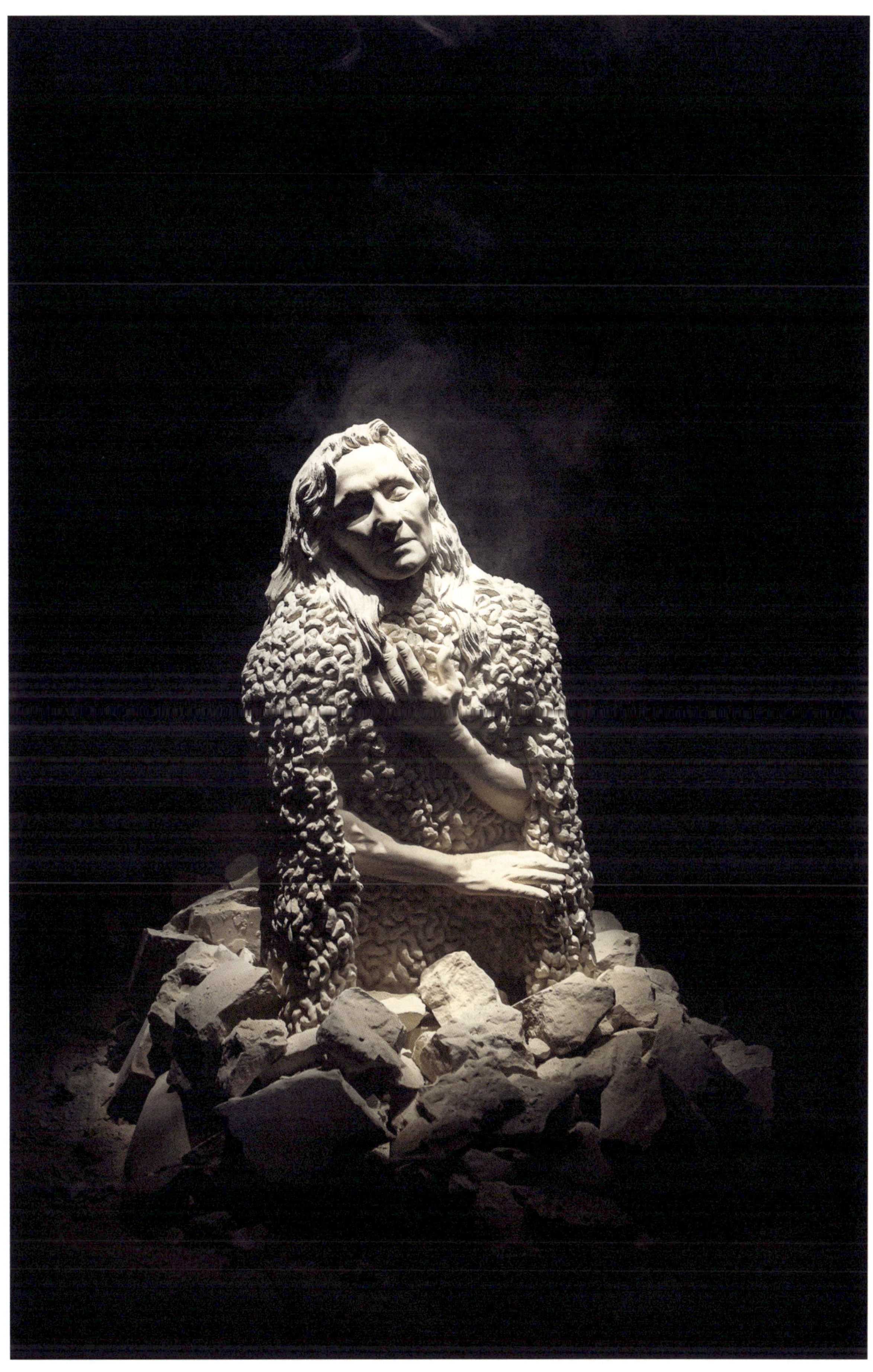

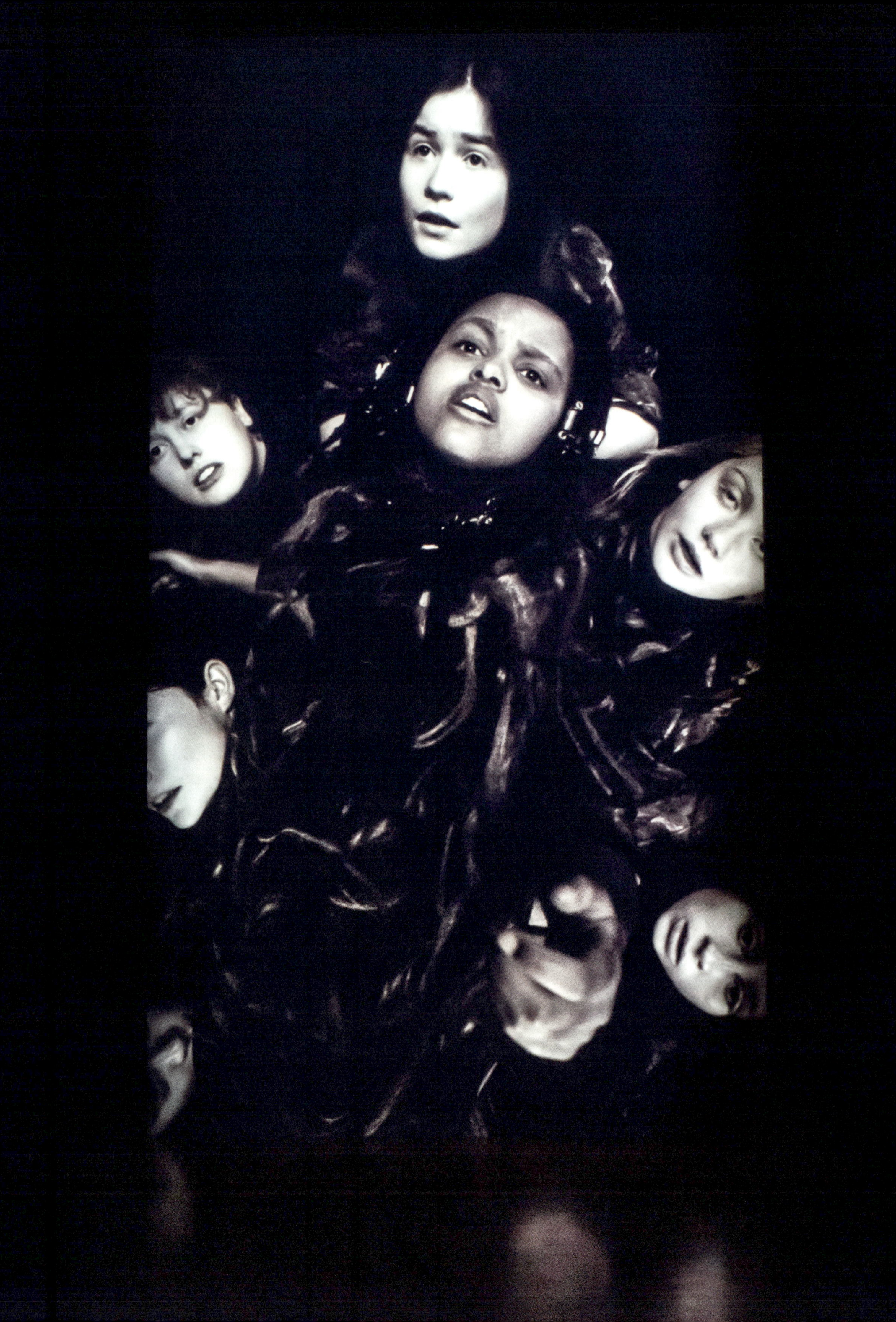

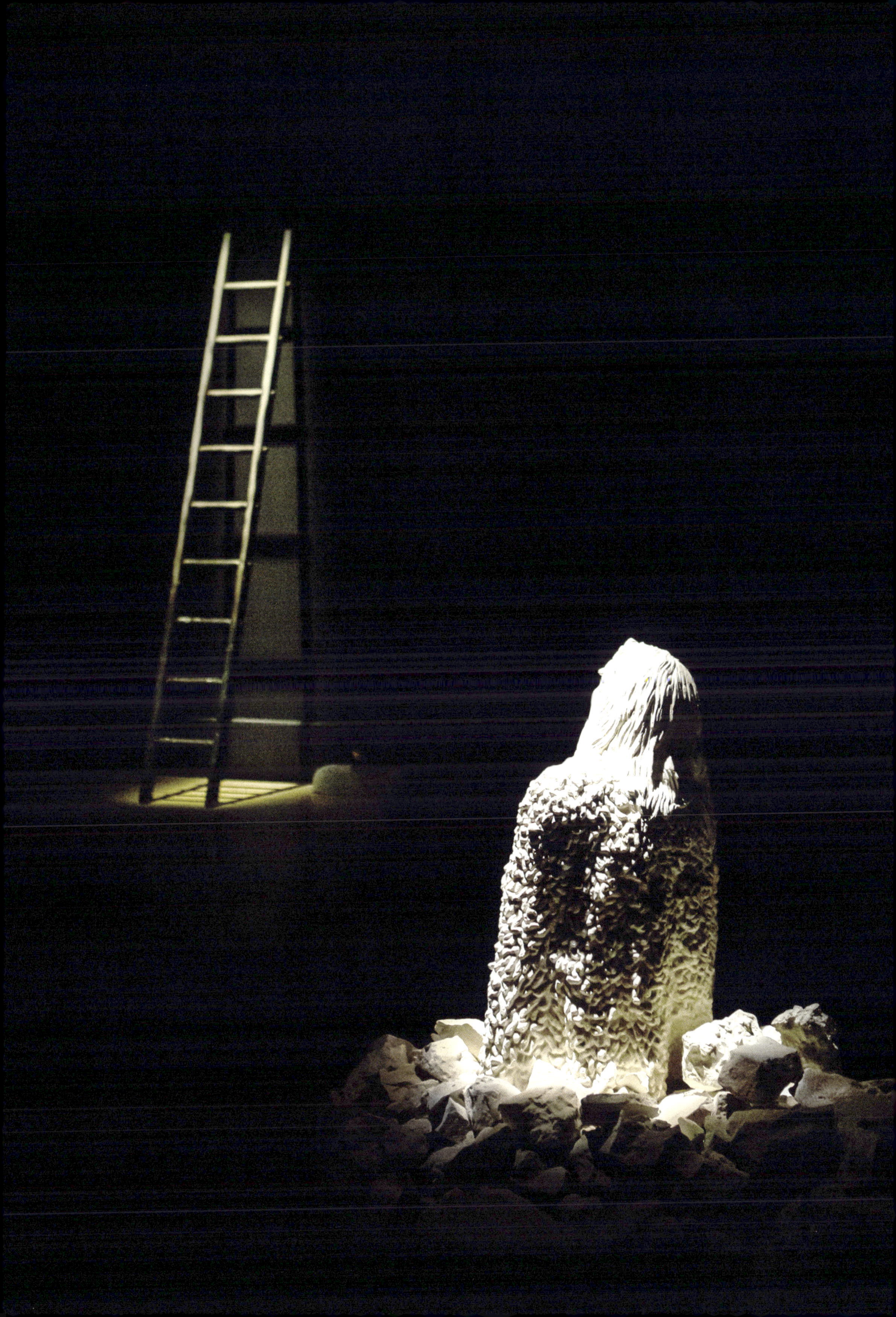

The darkness of an isolated cell, and the darkness of both *Tremble Tremble* and *The Tower* ... the liminality of darkness seems to have an intrinsic relationship to art.

TG      I remember the first conversations we had about *Tremble Tremble* were actually about its audience. How they would feel, what their sensory perception would be? Even then, it felt like a cave. And yet, it's fascinating to hear you speak of this cell and isolation, when we are now in post-pandemic times, but when the memory of touch being deprived is still so strong. In this cell, this room, there's a piece of stone in between, another kind of portal which allows the public to engage with the figure on the inside. What are you wanting this to activate within the work?

JJ      I am interested in hagioscopes. They can be found in the stone walls of a church – and served as a small opening that allowed the anchorite or penitent within a cell to witness a moment of significance in the church – the raising of the host, a moment of magic. It emerged in the post-plague period but is also called a 'leper's squint' in Scotland and the UK. This small hole or gap in a stone was the only opening to a cell that contained the body, sealing it off from the public. While the leper's body might be a contagion, their eye still holds the ability to receive and transmit. Within the cell in Edinburgh, viewed through our version of a hagioscope, will be a performer engaged in an activity – a daily studio practice – which is to create tiny little votives. A friend gave me a little Milagro after the opening in Venice and I kept it in my pocket for ages. I started to think of it as a little touchstone or magical material. Using spikenard, the oil of Mary Magdalene, as well as frankincense, I created little clay pieces with metal Milagros pressed inside them. It is a very modest gesture from my studio, a spell even, and becomes a shareable gift for the viewer.

When I first showed the work, the performers would share them by hand, through touch; a physical, material marker of that transactional body language between giving and receiving touch. It's something I've worked on before in a project with Sarah Browne called *The Touching Contract*. At what point do we negotiate touch with the other? The performer might push them through the hole

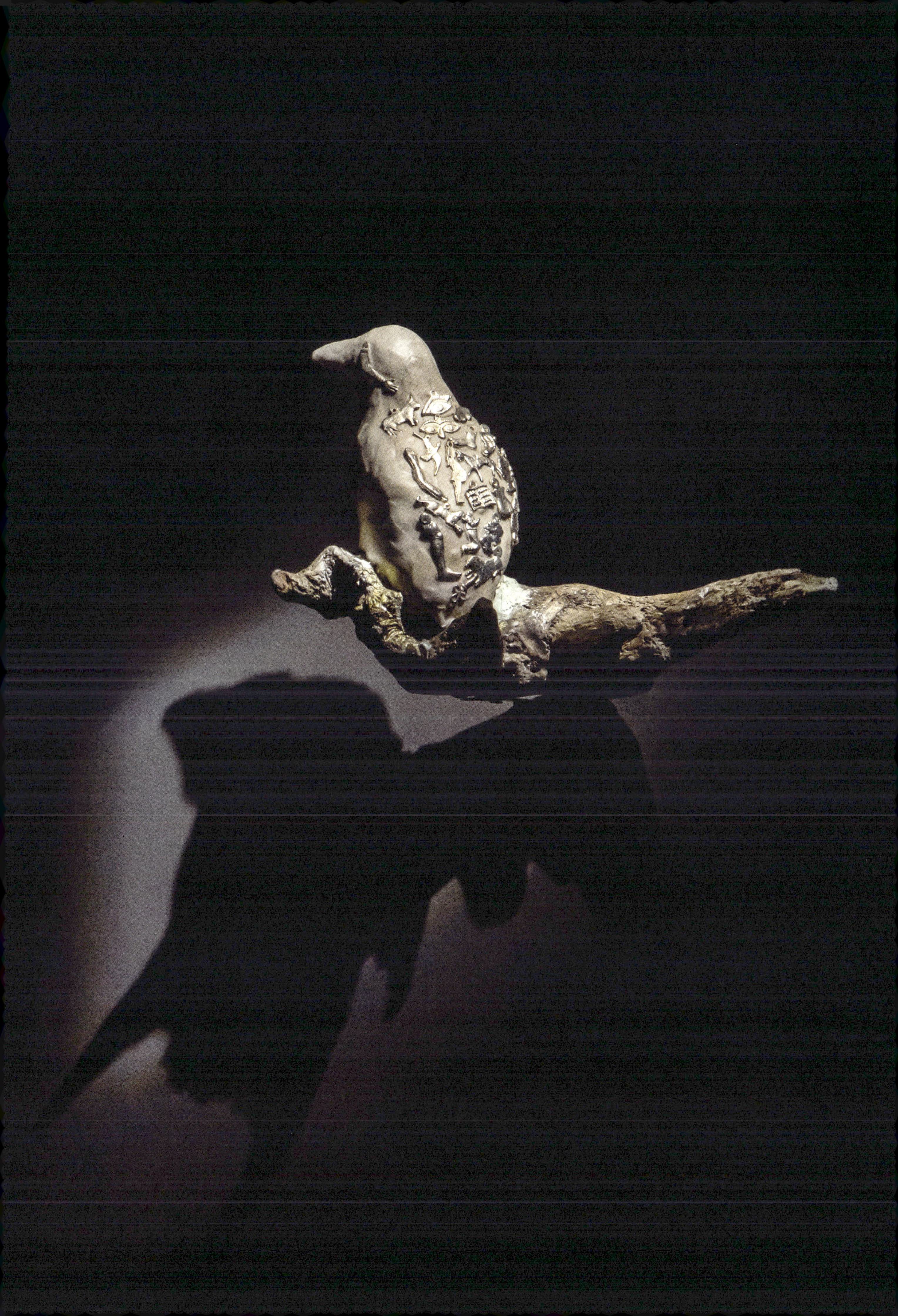

in the hagioscope, or approach the audience in the dark and give them a clay Milagro gift – like a contagion spreading through this modest little object. What is the space between the performer and the artwork and the audience? And how do you bridge that gap, or how do you find moments of transformation, or a kind of magic in the space between us and the artwork?

TG   The form of *Tremble Tremble* and *The Tower* are quite unusual for a gallery setting and indeed, for someone like you, an artist who's evolved out of the visual arts. You and I have called this at different times an expanded form of cinema or immersive theatre, or you could even call it performative installation. Although it still feels like it's slipping between all those gaps, which is possibly the product of contemporary culture delineating itself in a way that you're no longer constrained by, collaborating as you are with choreographers, musicians, theatre technicians, actors. However, I remember you once calling the form of *Tremble Tremble* an accumulation of runes. Can you describe what you mean by this?

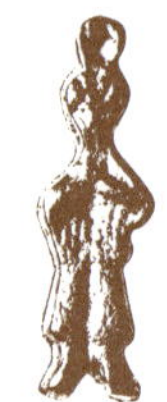

JJ   The accumulation of runes is also like tarot. When we were making *Tremble Tremble*, we spent a lot of time thinking about how the audience navigate the work – where they arrive, how they are moved through the duration of each segment. Rather than looking at the work as a series of objects or technologies, I started thinking about the artwork as a time event. That's why it resists all these formal categorisations. I think this connects to the storytelling environment I grew up in: my mum being a very powerful psychic and working through storytelling, tea-leaf reading, and that becoming a way that I learned about the event space of storytelling as a series of images or shadowy reflections, where one leads to another. It's the difference between story space and narrative – narrative being something that is imposed whereas the story space is the walking between moments, with enough looseness for not knowing.

TG   Most of the venues *Tremble Tremble* and *The Tower* have been presented in have been galleries. The one that was the most unknown was the technical theatre of Project Arts Centre in

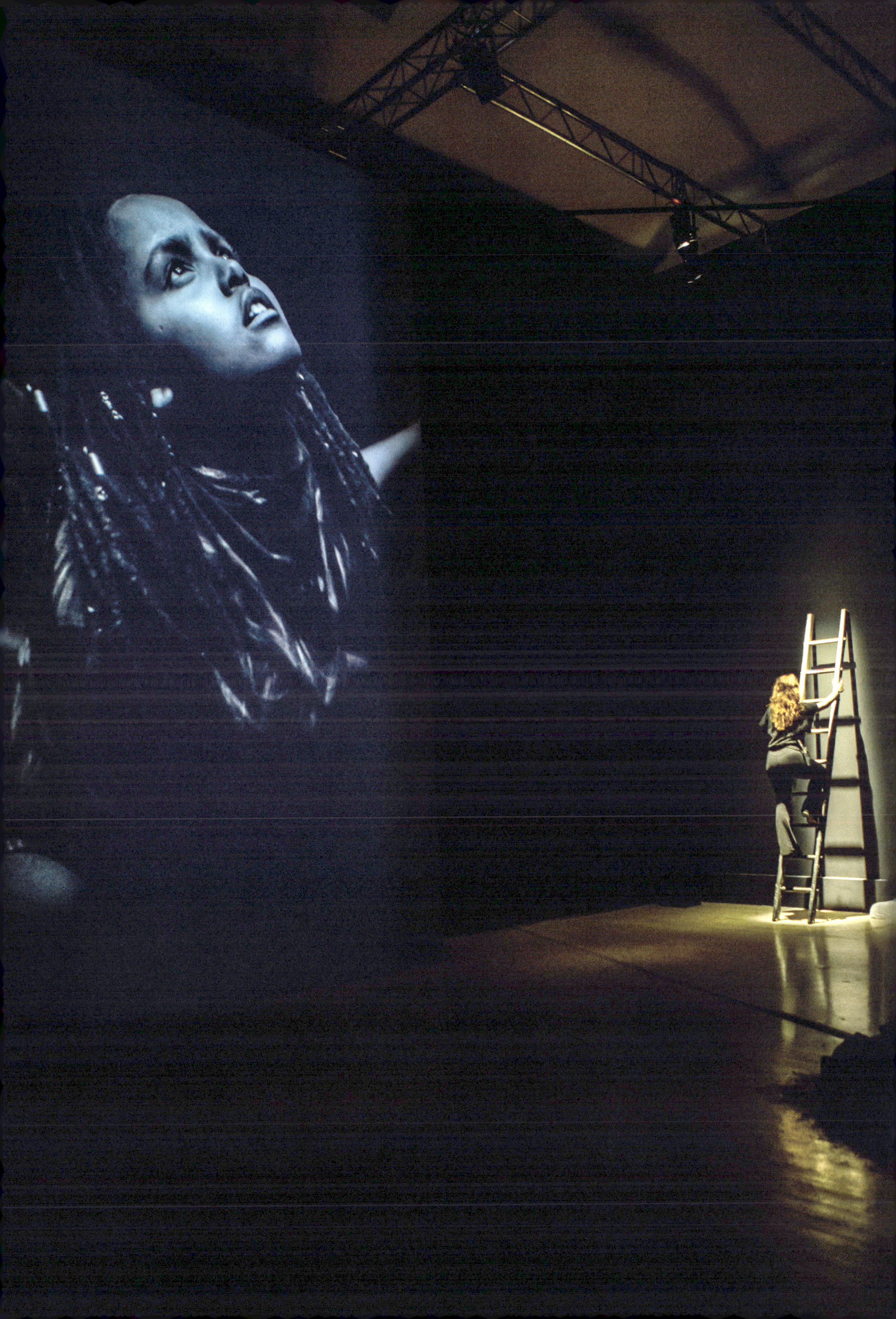

Dublin. So much of the apparatus of these artworks draws from theatre. But to *become* theatre, or to stage the exhibition in a theatre, we needed to go deeper. Not just allow the audience out of their seats but activate the apparatus of the building – the plumbing, the foundation stones beneath. This was when the millstone entered, and the performers drank from a tap at the wall.

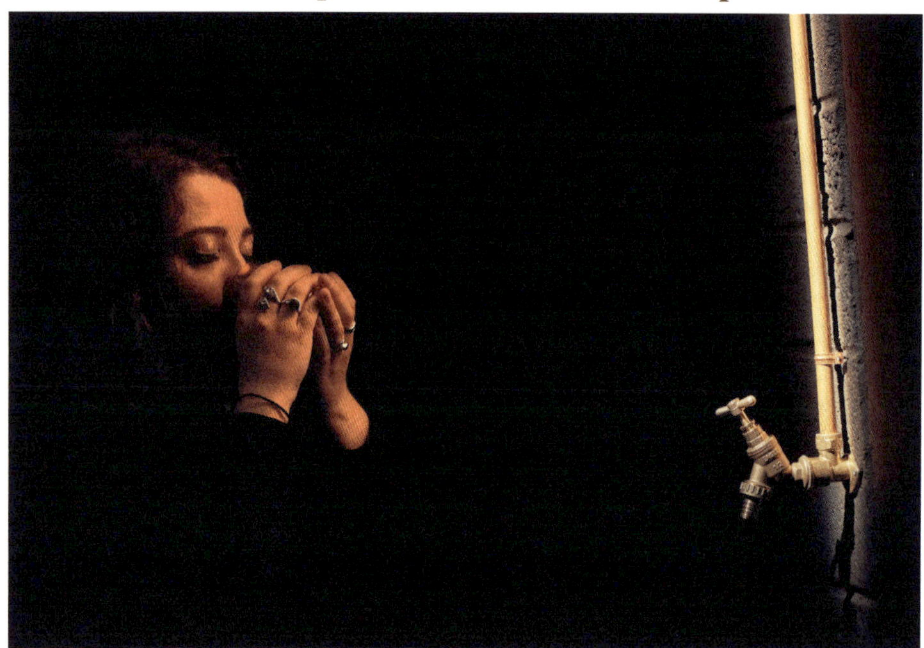

JJ There were a few magical aspects of that iteration. First of all, the timing was just incredibly magical. We had gone through this exhausting process of fighting for the repeal of the Eighth Amendment, and there was a sense of jubilance that we had gotten it over the line, but also shock and exhaustion. People were very moved to have been seen and recognised in such a deep and profound way by each other, by the community, by the nation as community.

The other part of the magic was that you and I had worked in that space together for 10 years. I made my first ever exhibition in the gallery of that building with you. I had just come out of art school and you had just started working in Project Arts Centre. I had not really thought of myself as a gallery-based artist. I was more interested in public art and activism, community and collaborative structures of art making. I didn't feel particularly attached to the gallery as a space. But you brought me to think about work existing in a gallery in a way that I would find meaningful in terms of politics. So, when we went back to do a show together 10 years later in Project, we had a very strong grounding of what we both really cared about and that was the political as a space of collective experience and ritual. By the time we were in this really intense political moment, we were also in the space that was at our home. And it was also Olwen Fouéré's home as she's performed countless times in that theatre. We were all at home.

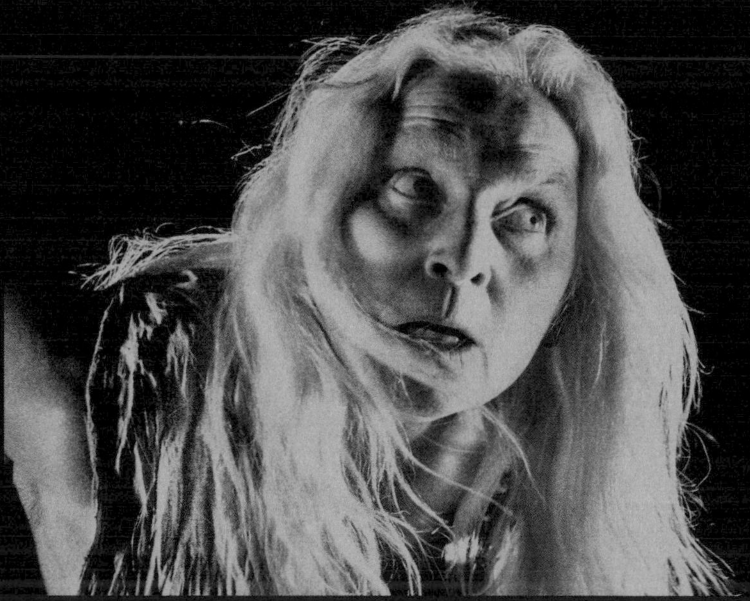

TG    As you talk about the performance of Olwen Fouéré, and earlier, when you reminded me that *Caliban and the Witch* is also very much at the root of this artwork, *The Tower*, I can't help but feel like there's a lot of Sylvia Federici's actual character in both of these performances that Olwen has undertaken.

JJ    I think it is interesting because Sylvia is a friend and has been such an important political touchstone in my work. When she came to Scotland to get her honorary doctorate, we snuck off to have some whisky in a pub and talked about both growing up under Catholicism, and how that has affected us as feminists. Sylvia is an incredibly profound activist and historian, but she also has an incredible artistic imaginary where something like *Caliban and the Witch* is thought of as an artistic space. I don't think it's a coincidence that she draws on Shakespeare and *The Tempest* as the staging for the story of *Caliban and the Witch* – she draws upon the theatrical. She draws on this when she talks about dancers and about artists.

**TG**  When making *Tremble Tremble* you were directly motivated by the mounting energy to give women back their bodily autonomy – to repeal the Eighth Amendment. *The Tower* continues this energy, but less in terms of changing the law, and more in terms of reckoning, reparations and apologies. If you extrapolate it from the Magdalene laundries, there's a broader implication for how we, how communities or nations account for historical atrocities, and the reparations that are needed to support the healing and undoing of a lot of patriarchal and colonial damage.

**JJ**  When I made *Tremble Tremble*, there was a direct consequence to conjuring the power of the law. We were engaged in a legal transformation as a nation. And the law was there as something that was, at that moment in time, *blocking* our entry into a subjective space of being. For example, when *Tremble Tremble* was in production in 2017, a woman or pregnant person had equal rights with her foetus. When I came to making *The Tower*, I wanted to deal with a different mode of body trauma – histories of institutional incarceration and violence – but in a way that doesn't stop us. I don't think that *The Tower* is presenting a solution in any way. But it was drilling into a potential space of the imaginary to move us through traumatic histories to new possibilities.

I think a lot of it came from being very isolated in the early stages of making the work. I was in Skibbereen, a town in the west of Ireland that was absolutely devastated in the mid-nineteenth century by an incredibly violent famine that was economic genocide – a deliberate decision by the British empire to export food while the country was starving. The stones echo with that resonance in the streets of Skibbereen. I was also reading Porete, Mechthild of Magdeburg and Julian of Norwich, and finding a connection between the medieval period, the process of economic and cultural colonisation and the impact it had on women's bodies. I was feeling these resonances, but at some stage in the research have to let go and allow for it to just be this mad thing that occupies and burrows into my own unconscious. That's what allows it to emerge in a different way for me as an artwork.

**TG** I remember when filming *Tremble Tremble*, you took the last 15 minutes of the day to shoot the scenes with Olwen that you called the 'Id'. This was separate from all the research, not representing anything, more like disruptors for the whole experience – but deliberately so.

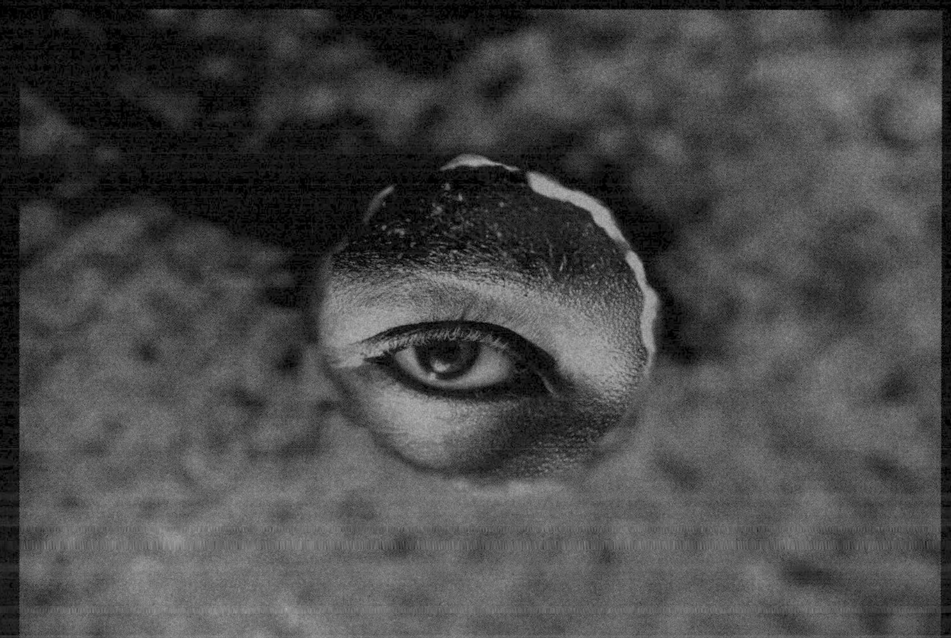

**JJ** I remember. I loved using those vignettes in the artwork. What is this thing that's disrupting or trying to bubble over and break through the rational production methodology of making a film? Allowing space for the unconscious to emerge is so important to me as an artist. And it's possible, if you have the right collaborators – like Olwen – who you're able to connect with in a tacit way. And I have that with you, where a tiny little kernel of a word becomes an idea really quickly, because there's a history of knowing each other's practices. The hagioscope that we developed for Talbot Rice, connects to ways we've worked together in the past, developing ways of thinking about the viewer and spectatorship, watching and looking. I remember one of the first shows that I saw that you made was the show with Aurélien [Froment] in 2007 at Project Arts Centre, where there was a projector that came through the wall as a device, and around that time we had a lot of discussion about devices of spectatorship – how images produce us just as we produce images? Having long-standing collaborations means that you have an ability to access the unconscious magic between people because it's already there, in the room, and it just takes a bit of conjuring to bring it out.

The designer Róisín Gartland is often another one of my first collaborators. And for the first time I worked with Irene Buckley on *The Tower*, who is a composer who has a thorough understanding of medieval music and Hildegard of Bingen, but brings it to a loose, experimental place as well. Emma Dalesman was the brilliant cinematographer again, and she really led the decision for *The Tower* to be monochromatic.

**TG** Throughout this journey you and I have often discussed the potential of art within a wider public discourse, a more expanded national conversation. But it's only really in 'the doing' that we can truly understand and even shape that. What has it felt like from your experience, over these last five years, to be an artist so involved in the evolution of Ireland's cultural identity?

**JJ** Politics has always been at the heart of why I ever wanted to make art. I've always cared about the sense of a shared political history, and always asked myself – what can art do in relationship to that? Over time I have become more confident in my vocabulary as an artist to allow for a space of experience, a shared narrative and an unconscious drive that we might all share. I've been really interested in this for a long time. About eight years ago I made a project in Korea called the *Psychic Reunification Project*. It was a tarot card reading with a gayageum performance on the border of North and South Korea, trying to speak to North Korea using shamanism and magical practice. It was staged as a press conference. I didn't do that just to make an artwork. A part of me and my collaborators did believe that we would find some communication, moment of enlightenment or knowledge that would connect. Kyungso Park is an incredible gayageum player. She repeated the same note over and over again, until a young child broke the silence, and asked 'will North and South Korea ever be reunited in my lifetime?' And the whole auditorium erupted with a kind of grief and a shame and a wonder that this child had asked this question. I feel that the role of art is to be a space for other kinds of political thinking. I would really fight for that, for my own practice and for any artist.

An artists' work – not just mine – can connect to something very deep within our culture, which is our shared experience and ability to articulate a sense of the unknown, a sense of the troubling of what the potential futures are or what the past is. And it is artists who do this troubling. They do the kind of work of the unconscious that is necessary for us to have a rational political collective strategy. After all, we've seen people from any moment of time through the art that they made. I think of the 'arm's length principle' of decision-making: the relationship of cultural bodies to the State that allowed us to make *Tremble Tremble* for the Irish Pavilion at Venice in the first place. At that time there was deep, deep sensitivity about abortion rights, and yet nothing about it was censored. We said exactly what we wanted to say – in the artwork, but also during all the protocol moments, standing next to the Ambassador. I think it really attests to the role of art as a space of freedom and experimentation, to take risks and to be playful, but also to ventilate necessary elements of our own collective unconscious that we have to understand in order to be political and have agency together.

If you look at Ireland over the last 10 years, we've had to negotiate ourselves in an intimate, democratic way, from marriage equality to Repeal. We've had to negotiate a kind of compassionate, subjective nationhood which hasn't always been easy. And perhaps we don't have as much polarisation as parts of the UK because we have experienced such an intimate oscillation of trying to change deeply-rooted historical concepts. And we were doing it intergenerationally. The result of all of this is that Ireland has developed a really interesting political and cultural landscape. We've gone through something quite profound in the last generation and decade, and this change is going to continue to evolve

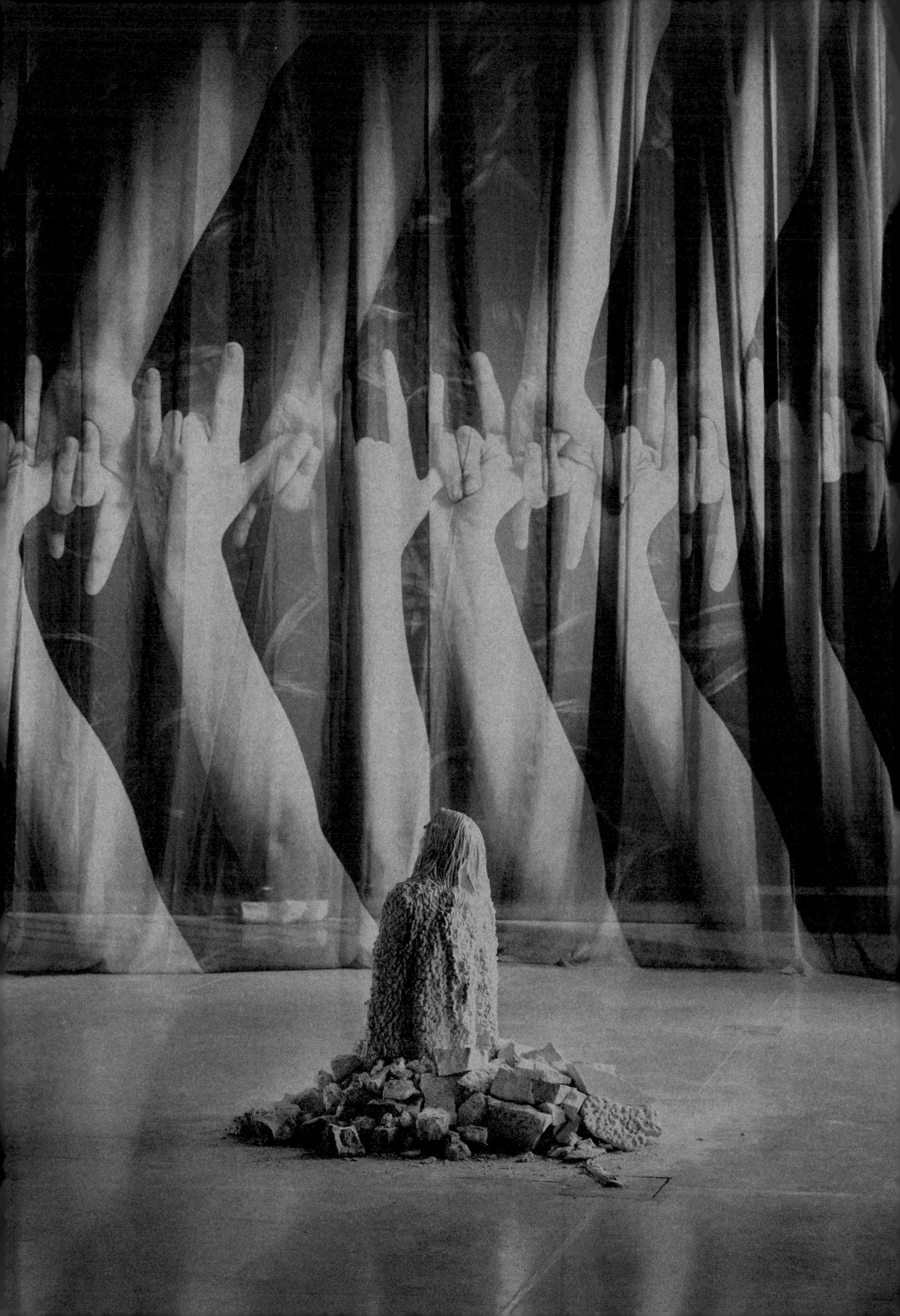

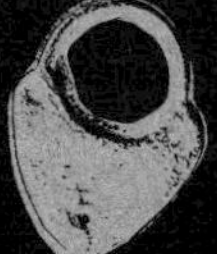

## TREMBLE TREMBLE

pp. 3, 6-7, 52
Ros Kavanagh

pp. 8, 21 (lower)
Sia Duff, Samstag Museum of Art,
University of South Australia, 2021

pp. 12-13, 14
Guggenheim Museum
Bilbao, 2019

pp. 10-11, 18-19,
28, 36, 60, 113, 114
Tessa Giblin

pp. 15, 16, 20, 24, 58-59
Sally Jubb, Talbot Rice Gallery,
Edinburgh, 2018

p. 21 (upper)
Weizhong Deng, ICA, LASALLE College
of the Arts, Singapore, 2017

pp. 22-23, 27, 34-35
Ros Kavanagh, Pavilion of Ireland at
the 57th Venice Biennale, 2017

p. 26
Jean de Heinzelin de Braucourt,
Royal Belgian Institute of
Natural Sciences, 1950

pp. 50-51, 112
Ros Kavanagh,
Project Arts Centre,
Dublin, 2018

p. 63
Maxwells
Photography

pp. 64-65
Christian Kerskens

pp. 93, 95
Jesse Jones

p. 96
Daily Record, 18 September 1958
©CSG CIC Glasgow Museums and Libraries Collection:
The Mitchell Library, Special Collections

p. 97
Illustration, p. 32 'Glasgow Charitable
and Philanthropic Institutions', 1892 / Glasgow
Caledonian University Archive Centre, Heatherbank
Social Work Collection, picture library print 6413

Milagros throughout photographed by
Jesse Jones and Chris Counihan

## THE TOWER

pp. 69, 70, 74, 75, 78, 88-89, 90, 98, 99,
100, 101, 102, 105, 106, 107, 109, 111, 115
Sally Jubb, Talbot Rice Gallery,
Edinburgh, 2023

pp. 83-84
Marion Burgin

p. 118
Ros Kavanagh,
Rua Red, Dublin, 2022

Our thanks to Jesse Jones, not only for continuing her incredible journey with us through *The Tower*, but also for being an inspirational leader and advocate for artists and cultural workers.

Thanks as always to our colleagues who support and champion the gallery's programme from across the University of Edinburgh and Edinburgh College of Art, particularly Professor Juan Cruz, Principal. And our long-term partners at Creative Scotland, with the support of Amanda Catto and Lottie Thorne.

We are grateful to Maolíosa Boyle and everyone at Rua Red for their support, to Culture Ireland for funding the work in Edinburgh – in particular Ciarán Walsh, and Tom Creed for his timely encouragement.

Thanks to Kim McAleese for her collaborative approach to Edinburgh Art Festival, and to the wonderful Naomi Moonveld-Nkosi for coming to Edinburgh to produce a youth workshop with the Festival.

Thanks also to everyone who has leaped in to support the making of the book – to Carol MacDonald at Edinburgh University Press for her bolstering enthusiasm; to Michael and Fraser at Fraser Muggeridge studio, for the creative juices and rigor which make these books such a joy to make together; to Miranda Blennerhassett for her consistency and precision; to all the writers – Tara Londi, Naomi Moonveld-Nkosi, Jessica Kennedy and Megan Kennedy, Lisa Godson, Tina Kinsella and Silvia Federici – who, as Jesse says in her interview with Tessa Giblin, is the 'spine of *Tremble Tremble* and *The Tower*'.

*The Tower* is one of the most complex projects we have presented at Talbot Rice Gallery, as was *Tremble Tremble*, and its success is a real credit to the ingenuity and determination of our technician, Colm Clarke, assisted by Tanith Marron. Special thanks to those who supported him: Giulia Gentili, Pavlos Georgiou, Luke Gregg, Hamish Halley, Jack Handscombe, Angus Hepburn, Jen Martin, Casey Miller, Lorenzo Robertson, Jessie Giovane Staniland. Thanks also to Michael Stapleton and Mark Murphy for being here in Edinburgh and their continuing work on *The Tower*. Many thanks to Sally Jubb for installation photography.

As always, thanks to our community partners and our fabulous volunteers, who bring our exhibitions to life.

Director: Tessa Giblin
Deputy Director: Melissa MacRobert
Gallery Technician: Colm Clarke
Assistant Technician: Tanith Marron

Supported by the rest of the TRG team:
James Clegg
Rue Cooper
Chris Counihan
Vira Putri
Monika Stepanikova

## JESSE JONES

Jesse Jones is a Dublin-based artist. She represented Ireland at the 57th Venice Biennale in 2017 with the work *Tremble Tremble*, which toured to ICA LASALLE College of Arts, Singapore (2017); Project Arts Centre, Dublin (2018); Talbot Rice Gallery, University of Edinburgh (2018-19); Museo Guggenheim Bilbao (2019-2020) and SAMSTAG Museum of Art and the Adelaide Art Festival (2021). Recent solo exhibitions include *The Tower* at Rua Red, Tallaght (2022) and *Syllabus*, a five-year project commissioned by Kunsthal Gent, Belgium (2020-2025). Other solo exhibitions include *NO MORE FUN AND GAMES*, Dublin City Gallery, The Hugh Lane, Dublin (2016); *The Other North*, Art Sonje Centre, Seoul (2013); CCA Londonderry (2013); *Sleepwalkers*, Hugh Lane Municipal Art Gallery, Dublin (2012); *The Struggle Against Ourselves*, Spike Island, Bristol; REDCAT Los Angeles (2011); The National Sculpture Factory, Cork (2011); Blackwood Gallery, University of Toronto (2009); *The Spectre and the Sphere*, Project Arts Centre, Dublin (2008).

Group exhibitions include *Bones in the Attic*, Hugh Lane Gallery, Dublin (2022); *COME ALIVE*, Het Nieuwe Muntgebouw, Utrecht (2022); *The Other Side - Borderlands in Contemporary Irish Art*, Dortmunder U, Dortmund (2019-20); *Gaia Has 1000 Names*, Elgiz Museum, Istanbul (2019); *At The Gates*, La Criée centre d'art contemporain, Rennes (2019); *Still I Rise*, Nottingham Contemporary and De La Warr Pavilion, Bexhill-on-Sea (2019); *Mademoiselle*, Centre régional d'art contemporain (CRAC) de Sète (2018); *Against the Romance of Community*, Swiss Institute, New York (2016), *Radical Actions*, RMIT Gallery, Melbourne (2016); *The Eclipse of an Innocent Eye*, National Gallery, Prague (2015); *Primal Architecture*, IMMA, Dublin (2015); *Ghosts, Spies, and Grandmothers*, Seoul Media City Biennial, Seoul Museum of Art (2014); *Invisible Violence*, Museum of Contemporary Art, Belgrade and ARTIUM, Basque country; *The Talking Cure*, Oakville Galleries Toronto and IMA Brisbane (2014). Jones also produced the major public art project *In the Shadow of the State* with Sarah Browne, commissioned by Artangel.

Her work is in collections of the Irish Museum of Modern Art, Dublin City Gallery, Hugh Lane Gallery and University of Edinburgh Art Collection. She is the 250th member of Aosdána, founded in 1981 to honour artists whose work has made an outstanding contribution to the creative arts in Ireland. She lectures in Fine Art at Technological University Dublin. Jones has a forthcoming solo exhibition at IKON Gallery, Birmingham in 2024.

## SILVIA FEDERICI

Silvia Federici is a long-time activist, teacher, historian and writer. In 1972 she was one of the founders of the International Feminist Collective, the organisation that launched the Campaign for Wages for Housework in the US and abroad. She is the author of many essays on political philosophy, feminist theory, cultural studies, and has lectured in universities in the US, Europe, Africa and South America. Her published works include *Revolution at Point Zero* (2012) and *Caliban and the Witch: Women, the Body and Primitive Accumulation* (2004). In 2019 she was awarded an honorary degree by the University of Edinburgh for her tireless vocal opposition to societal injustices including patriarchal exploitation, gender imbalance and racial discrimination. Federici is Emerita Professor of Political Philosophy and International Studies at Hofstra University, New York.

## TESSA GIBLIN

Professor Tessa Giblin is the Director of Talbot Rice Gallery at the University of Edinburgh, where she holds a Personal Chair in Contemporary Curating with Edinburgh College of Art. At TRG she has curated exhibitions of Céline Condorelli (UK/Italy), Emeka Ogboh (Nigeria), Angelica Mesiti (Australia), Samson Young (Hong Kong), Lucy Skaer (Scotland) and Jesse Jones (Ireland). Recent group exhibitions have included *The Normal* (reflecting on the impact of the pandemic), *Borderlines* (art in the age of Brexit), *At the Gates* (on women and power) and *Riddle of the Burial Grounds* (art in relation to the Anthropocene and nuclear waste burial). She has been a judge for the Paul Hamlyn Foundation Awards for Visual Arts, selection committee for Scotland+Venice and part of the acquisitions committee for the Frac Bretagne 2020-22. From 2006-16 Giblin was curator of Project Arts Centre in Ireland where she produced more than 60 solo and group exhibitions, as well as being Commissioner and Curator for Ireland at Venice with Jesse Jones in 2017. She is originally from Aotearoa/New Zealand.

## LISA GODSON

Lisa Godson is a cultural historian with a focus on material culture including ritual, medical instruments and 'tropical' modern architecture. She is director of the MA in Design History and Material Culture at the National College of Art and Design, Dublin. Her books include *Uniform: Clothing and Discipline in the Modern World* (2019); *Modern Religious Architecture in Germany, Ireland and Beyond* (2019); *Making 1916: Visual and Material Culture of the Easter Rising* (2015); *The Secret Lives of Objects* (2015). She has undertaken a number of collaborations with artists including with Still Films on the documentary feature *Build Something Modern*, based on her research into modernist architecture in West Africa, and Jesse Jones for the Irish pavilion at the Venice Biennale. Her monograph *How the Crowd Felt: Public Ritual, Memory and Space* is forthcoming. Her current publication project is a critical material history of the Royal Hospital Kilmainham/Irish Museum of Modern Art.

## JUNK ENSEMBLE

Junk Ensemble is a multi-award-winning Dublin-based dance theatre company founded by twin sisters Megan Kennedy and Jessica Kennedy. The company is committed to engaging diverse audiences through the creation and presentation of brave, imaginative and accessible work that sheds light on important human issues relevant to society today. Current Associate Artists at Project Arts Centre and previous Artists-in-Residence at the Tate, London, Junk Ensemble has built a reputation as one of Ireland's leading voices in dance. Junk Ensemble frequently collaborates with artists from other disciplines to produce a rich mix of visual and performance styles that challenge the traditional audience/performer relationship. This approach has led to productions being created in non-traditional or found spaces as well as more conventional theatre spaces. The company often works directly with communities in the creation and performance of their work. Their work has toured to New York, Europe, the UK and Ireland.

## TINA KINSELLA

Dr Tina Kinsella is Head of Design and Visual Arts at the Institute of Art, Design and Technology, Dublin, and Research Fellow at the Centre for Gender and Women's Studies, Trinity College Dublin. She is Principal Investigator for *Feminist Art Making Histories* (FAMH), an oral history, digital humanities research project funded by the Irish Research Council and the Arts and Humanities Research Council, UK (2021-2024). She regularly collaborates with contemporary artists, such as Bracha L. Ettinger, Alice Maher, Aideen Barry, Sarah Browne and Jesse Jones. Her most recent curatorial project, *Fair is Foul & Foul is Fair*, was shown at the Katzen Arts Center, American University, Washington DC in 2019. She is particularly interested in surrealism and its legacies and has published on artists associated with this movement, including Leonora Carrington, Frida Kahlo and Francesca Woodman. She is an elected member of the *Association Internationale des Critiques d'Art*.

## TARA LONDI

Tara Londi is an Italian-Irish curator, art critic and writer, born in Rome and based in London. Tara is a graduate of Goldsmiths University of London and has worked in the UK, France, USA, Latin America and Asia. Her projects extend from exhibitions to cultural programmes, film festivals, documentaries and philanthropy. Among her most recent exhibitions, *Gaia Has 1000 Names* (Istanbul, 2019) inspired numerous institutional programmes on the relationship between women, ecology and capitalism. Tara is the author of *Ecofeminist Art: on the Concept of Heritage* (Postmedia Press, Milan, 2023).

## NAOMI MOONVELD-NKOSI

Naomi Moonveld-Nkosi is a young writer, performer and artist from Dublin. Naomi has been actively engaging with The Ark Children's Council since 2017 and is currently an alumni member. She collaborated on the work *What Did I Miss?* by Shaun Dunne (2018-2020) which was performed at The Ark during the pandemic. In 2022 she collaborated with Jesse Jones on a film installation called *The Tower* as part of the Magdalene Series commissioned by Rua Red. She has also hosted a conversation and presentation with Jones on the archetype of the witch in the Viernulvier Women and Children First Festival. Naomi is currently collaborating with Jesse Jones on a new work entitled *Witch Story*, commissioned as the first equal co-creation between a child and an adult artist at Ireland's national children's cultural centre The Ark.

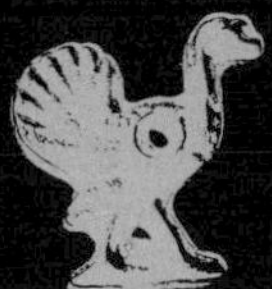

# Tremble Tremble

*Tremble Tremble* was commissioned and curated by Talbot Rice Gallery Director, Tessa Giblin, for Ireland at Venice, an initiative of Culture Ireland in partnership with the Arts Council, for the 57th Venice Biennale in 2017.

*Tremble Tremble* was originally produced and supported by Project Arts Centre. Principal Sponsor: Dublin Port Company. International Partner: LASALLE College of the Arts, Singapore. Production Partner: Institute of Art, Design + Technology (IADT). Proudly supported by CIT Crawford College of Art & Design; Talbot Rice Gallery, Edinburgh College of Art and the University of Edinburgh; South Dublin County Council and Rua Red; Dublin City Council; Dublin City Gallery The Hugh Lane; the Irish Museum of Modern Art. The presentation in Edinburgh was supported by Creative Scotland, and Culture Ireland as part of GB18: Promoting Irish Arts in Britain.

| | |
|---|---|
| Artist: | Jesse Jones |
| Performer & Artistic Collaborator: | Olwen Fouéré |
| Sound Design & Composition: | Susan Stenger |
| Production Manager & AV Programmer: | Aaron Kelly |
| Exhibition Dramaturg: | Tessa Giblin |
| Object Fabrication: | Rachel Fallon, James L Hayes, Catriona Gilbert |
| Printmaker: | Danielle Neville |

## PERFORMERS

| | |
|---|---|
| SAMSTAG, Adelaide: | Eleanor Amor |
| | Emily Clinton |
| | Sam Gold |
| | Olivia Kathigitis |
| Guggenheim Bilbao: | Estibaliz Ibarra Arriolabengoa |
| | Silvia Coppola |
| | Olatz Otalora |
| | Karmele Ugalde |
| Talbot Rice Gallery, University of Edinburgh: | Katie Dibb |
| | Tamara Elkins |
| | Fiona Halliday |
| | Connie Hurley |
| Project Arts Centre, Dublin: | Sara Grice |
| | Jesse Jones |
| | Sara O'Rourke |
| | Donna Rose |
| LASALLE College of the Arts, Singapore: | Chua Pei Yun |
| | Valerie Lim |
| | Isabel Phua |
| | Nur Afiqah Rapee |
| | Vanessa Tan |
| | Vasantha Tan |
| with thanks to: | Susan Sentler |

| | |
|---|---|
| Venice Biennale 2017: | Sara Grice |
| | Niamh Moloney |
| | Sara O'Rourke |
| | Catherine Byrne |
| | Clare Breen |
| | Niamh Moriarty |
| | Nicole Flanagan |
| | Irene Berkery |
| | Donna Rose |

## FILM PRODUCTION CREDITS

| | |
|---|---|
| Director: | Jesse Jones |
| Director of Photography: | Emma Dalesman |
| Assistant Director: | Tessa Giblin |
| Production Assistant: | Deborah Madden |
| Editor: | Eavan Aiken |
| Costume Designer: | Róisín Gartland |
| Stylist: | Alison Conneely |
| Miniatures Prop Maker: | John Garvey |
| Set: | Geoff Wilson, Wilson's Yard, Newry |
| Digital Imaging Technician: | Eavan Aiken |
| Focus Puller: | Alfie Hollingsworth |
| Grip and Jib Operator: | Roman Bugovdkiy |
| Sound Recordist: | Fiachra O'Hanlon |
| Sound Design: | Mark Murphy |
| Sound Consultant: | Killian Fitzgerald |
| Additional Sound: | Robert Poss |
| Gaffer: | Paul Noble |
| Sparks: | Aaron Kelly, Simon Burke |
| IADT Technician: | David Cooper |
| Continuity: | Sara O'Rourke |
| Catering: | Fiona Hallinan |
| Location Coordinator: | Jessica Fuller, Head of Creative Engagement, IADT |
| Legal Research: | Máiréad Enright, Senior Lecturer in Law, Birmingham Law School |
| Assistants: | Ciara Furlong |
| | Stephen Gilroy |
| | Elena Horgan |
| | Ash Middleton |
| | Darren Moynagh |
| | Lorcan Murphy |
| | Ellen O'Connor |
| | Brian O'Neill |
| | Sarah Whelan |
| Research Advisors: | Lisa Godson |
| | Tina Kinsella |
| | Kate Butler |
| Photography: | Ros Kavanagh |
| Producer: | Project Arts Centre |

*The Tower* was commissioned by Rua Red in Dublin as part of The Magdalene Series curated by Maolíosa Boyle, funded by The Arts Council of Ireland, Creative Ireland, South Dublin County Arts Office, and Rua Red. It has been further developed at Talbot Rice Gallery with the support of Creative Scotland, Edinburgh College of Art, Culture Ireland and Ron Christaldi.

## PERFORMERS

Olwen Fouéré
Naomi Moonveld-Nkosi
Emily Kilkenny Roddy
Ava Richards
Síofra Kildee-Doolan
Rosie Phipps O'Neill
Amy Sheil
Aedín Ferguson
Saoirse McSharry
Blathnaid Doyle Fox

Choreography: Junk Ensemble:
Jessica Kennedy and
Megan Kennedy
Live activation: Claudia Andrei Hartl
Fibi Cowley
Alliyah Enyo
Elisabeth Landgraf
Adélie Moye
Aniela Piasecka
Cathy Rowsome
Nina Willims

Featuring text adapted from Hildegard of Bingen (1098-1179) *Lingua Ignota, Scivias*; Marguerite Porete (1250-1310) *The Mirror of Simple Souls*; Mechthild of Magdeburg (c. 1207 – c. 1282/1294) *The Flowing Light of the Godhead.*

Texts adapted and selected by Olwen Fouéré, Jesse Jones and Naomi Moonveld-Nkosi

Composer: Irene Buckley
Sound Design: Mark Murphy
Sound Technician: Ian McNulty
Choir Master: Blánaid Murphy
Choir Manager: Germaine Carlos
*O Virtus Sapientiae* by Hildegard of Bingen

Costume Designer: Róisín Gartland
Wardrobe Department: Alison Conneely
Sara O'Rourke
Producer: Zlata Filipović
Production Manager: Jo Halpin
1st Assistant Director: Niall Owens
2nd Assistant Director: Bríanna Ní Léanacháin
Runner: Elena Larionova
Technical Consultant: Aaron Kelly
Q-lab and Sequencing: Michael Stapleton
Director of Photography: Emma Dalesman
1st Assistant Camera: Camila Gomes
2nd Assistant Camera: Katelyn Markham
O'Halloran

3rd Assistant Camera: Leon McCullough
Gaffer: Noel Greene
Assistant Gaffer: Maiya Rice
Jib Operator/Grip/Movi: Roman Bugovskiy
VFX Supervisor/DIT: Eavan Aiken
Assistant DIT: Hana Mohamed
Nasr El Din
Sound Recordist: Trevor Cunningham
Editor: Eavan Aiken
VFX: Enda O'Connor
Hair and Makeup Lead: Natalie Kinsella
Hair and Makeup: Klaudia Rapala
Saoirse Whelan
Hair and Makeup Assistant: Caroline Mackey
with thanks to: Clare Barman, IADT

## NATIONAL FILM SCHOOL, IADT

Paul Tynan, Technician, Department of Film + Media
David Cooper, Lecturer, Department of Film + Media
Jean Rice, Chair of Film + TV, Department of Film + Media
Vanessa Gildea, Head of Department Film + Media

Studio Engineer: Mark Bayley
Stunt Safety and
Rigging Team: Giedrius 'Gee' Nagys
Brendan Condron
Jokubus 'Jack' Nagys

Portland Stone Sculpture: S. McConnell and Sons:
Glynn Lucas
Declan Grant
Colin Lavery
Alan McConnell
Ian Nicholson
Pillar: 3D Printing Ireland Ltd:
Keith Davis
Kevin De Burca
Gavin Flanagan
Alan Davis
JSD Engineering: Stephen Davis and
John Staunton
Curtain: Showtex with
photography by
Ros Kavanagh and
Marion Bergin
Ladder: Spaceforms Ltd:
Sara Murphy
Bowl: Sam Gold
Stone Hagioscope: Colm Clarke
Lorenzo Robertson

Water Remedy designed by Sara O'Rourke
Spikenard, Frankincense, well water from
Tobar Fláinn, Brandon, Co. Kerry

*The Tower* font creative direction by Keith Nally, designed by Bobby Tannam

Published by Talbot Rice Gallery
University of Edinburgh
on the occasion of
Jesse Jones' exhibition *The Tower*
24 June – 30 September 2023

Curated by Professor Tessa Giblin,
Director of Talbot Rice Gallery

Talbot Rice Gallery
The University of Edinburgh
Old College, South Bridge
Edinburgh, EH8 9YL
United Kingdom

Front cover: Sally Jubb
Back cover and endpapers: Ros Kavanagh



Editors: Tessa Giblin and Melissa MacRobert
Design: Michael Kelly and Fraser Muggeridge
at Fraser Muggeridge studio
Print production: Graphius
Copyediting: Miranda Blennerhassett

Published by Talbot Rice Gallery
in partnership with
Edinburgh University Press
University of Edinburgh, 2023

Printed in Belgium
Edition of 1000

ISBN 978-1-7390838-5-4

The publishers would like to thank all those who
have given their kind permission to reproduce
material for this book. Every effort has been made
to achieve permission for the images in this catalogue,
however the publisher remains available in case
preliminary agreements were not able to be made
with copyright holders.

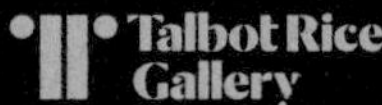
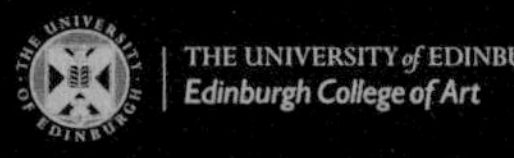
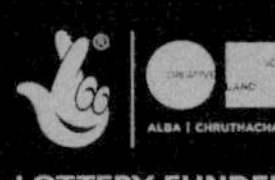
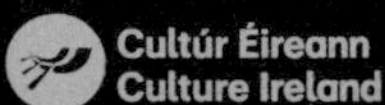
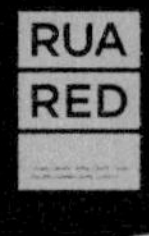
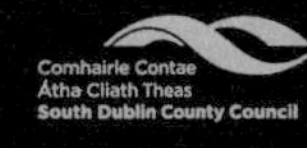
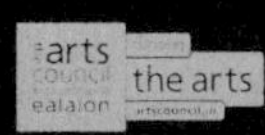
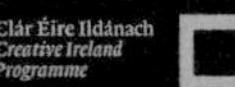
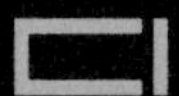

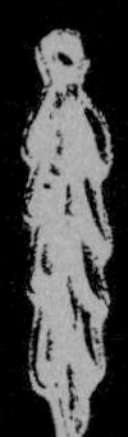

'In Praise of the Dancing Body' by Silvia Federici,
'O Children in God's Name Slay Not Your Mother!' by
Tina Kinsella, 'A Finger, a Hand-breadth, a Span, a Foot'
by Lisa Godson and 'Tremble Tremble' by Tessa Giblin
were originally published in *Tremble Tremble – Jesse
Jones* on the occasion of Ireland at Venice: the Pavilion
of Ireland at the 57th Venice Biennale by Project Press
(Project Arts Centre), Dublin and Mousse Publishing,
Milan, May 2017.

'Did We Disturb You Good People?' by Tessa Giblin was
commissioned in response to the exhibition 'Bones in
the Attic' at the Hugh Lane Gallery, Dublin, 11 August –
30 October 2022.

'The Tower' by Tara Londi, Junk Ensemble's text and
'The Void' by Naomi Moonveld-Nkosi were originally
published in 'The Tower' on the occasion of Jesse Jones'
exhibition at Rua Red, South Dublin Arts Centre,
27 May – 24 September 2022.

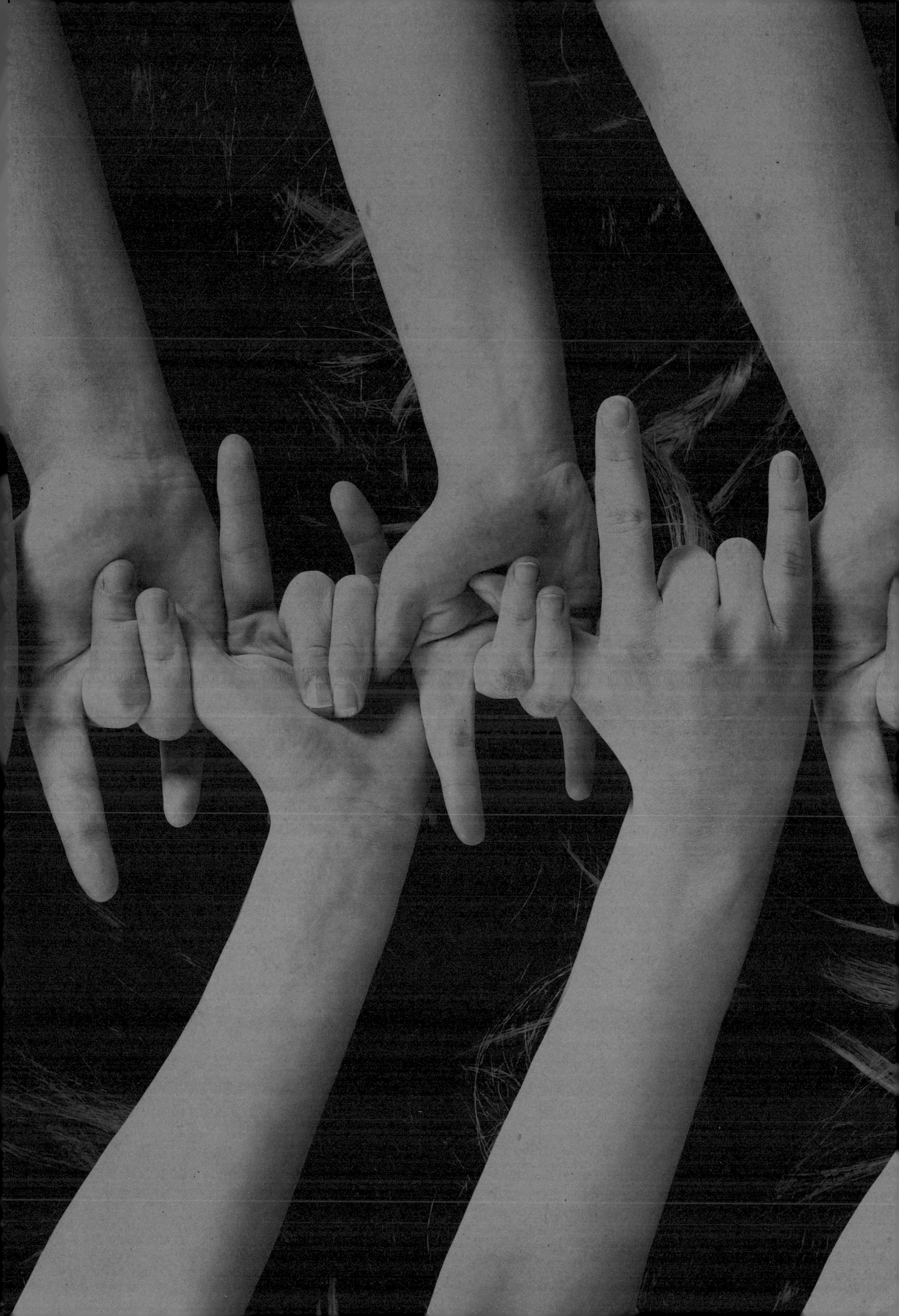

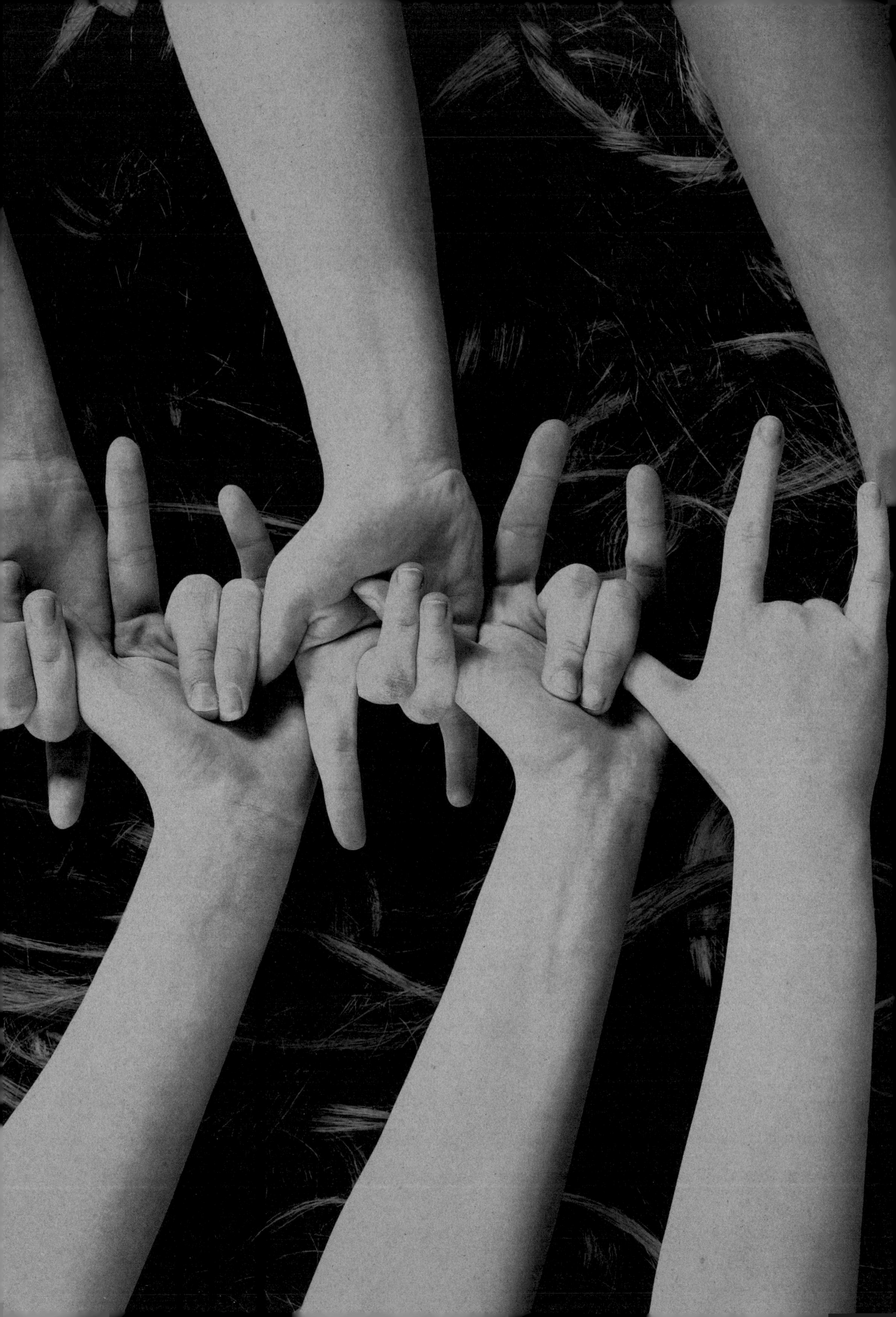